Dan Gook
Guide to Ncurses
Programming

Dan Gookin's Guide to Ncurses Programming
Written by Dan Gookin

Published by Quantum Particle Bottling Co.,
Coeur d'Alene, ID, 83814
USA

For additional information on this or other publications from Dan Gookin and Quantum Particle Bottling Co., please visit
http://www.wambooli.com/

Edition 1.0
September 2017

Table of Contents

Introduction

Nurses is a C (and Python) library that provides direct control over a terminal window. You use the library to control the cursor, place text in specific spots on the screen, and interactively read the keyboard.

This book presents an up-and-running tutorial that covers the basics of the Ncurses library, including input/output, text attributes, special characters, windows, pads, and mouse input.

Assumptions

Ncurses runs in a terminal environment, text mode. This environment can be found on most operating systems, specifically Linux, Mac OS X, and other POSIX systems. Windows features a terminal environment, though to make Ncurses happen you need a POSIX shell like Cygwin.

The terminal window doesn't need to be full-screen. Any terminal window in a GUI works.

Further, you must install the Ncurses library. Use the operating system's package manager to perform the setup, though the binaries and source can be found at http://invisible-island.net/ncurses/ncurses.html

Curses or Ncurses?

Curses has been around since the early 1980s. It was part of older versions of Unix, many of which came with complex licensing. An update to Curses was dubbed New Curses, or Ncurses, to avoid various copyright and legal issues.

In this book, I use the convention Ncurses, but internally the program is still Curses and the header and library files are named accordingly. Aliases for `ncurses -> curses` exist, so you can use either one.

The book is current with Ncurses version 6.0.

Conventions

This eBook uses the following conventions:

C language keywords and function names are shown in italic text, such as *newwin()* or *int*.

Variables and filenames are shown in blue monospaced text, such as `a` and `ncurses.h`.

Functions are introduced in this format:

`wrefresh(win)`

Program code appears with the source filename first, followed by the code:

00-01_box.c

```
1    #include <ncurses.h>
2
3    int main()
4    {
5        initscr();
6
7        box(stdscr,'*','*');
8        refresh();
9        getch();
10
11       endwin();
12       return(0);
13   }
```

The source filename uses chapter number, sequential number, followed by a unique name.

The line numbers to the left of the bar are for reference only; do not type them into your code.

The demonstration programs in this book are short and to the point. As such, they rarely include comments.

Later code examples dispense with some error-checking, primarily to keep the code short. The text points out when I omit the error-checking code, and I strongly recommend that you always check for errors in your own programs.

Source code and other resources are available on the companion website:

http://www.c-for-dummies.com/ncurses

Mise en place

This book was written on an iMac running OS X 10.12.5 and Ncurses version 6.0.20160910. Programs were tested on a Windows 7 PC running Cygwin, as well as an Ubuntu Linux system. Despite the different environments, Ncurses behaves consistently, especially when compiling and running the short sample code presented in this eBook.

Contacting the Author

Here is my real e-mail address:

dgookin@wambooli.com

I cannot promise to answer all e-mail, as I get a ton of it. Also, I do not provide technical support nor can I write code for you. I am more than happen, however, to help with issues specific to this eBook.

Enjoy Ncurses!

Dan Gookin
September 2017

1. The Set Up

This chapter covers a basic setup and organization for you to get started with Ncurses programming. My goal is to show how everything works and to get you comfortable with programming with Ncurses, even if you've never written a terminal (text mode) program before.

Ncurses is a Unix Thing

Ncurses was developed in the Unix environment to allow full-screen control over text programming. It exists primarily in Unix, though you can obtain a version for the Cygwin terminal that runs under Windows.

To obtain the current or updated release of Ncurses, use the package manager that comes with your operating system. For Linux, for example, use apt, the Advanced Package Tool. For OS/X, I recommend Homebrew. With Cygwin, use the Setup program you downloaded to install Cygwin.

The Terminal

As a text-mode toolkit, Ncurses operates in a terminal window or full-screen if you dare to start your computer in text mode. (It's possible.) Nearly every Unix implementation features a Terminal program, which displays text in a window. This is the environment in which Ncurses code runs.

Terminals come in different types, and the type of terminal used can affect how Ncurses behaves. I recommend using the standard xterm-color terminal to get the most from Ncurses. Type `echo $TERM` at the prompt to determine which terminal type is currently set. Refer to the terminal program window's settings or preferences to select a different type.

The terminal type `cygwin` is okay for that environment, though reading mouse input may be problematic.

1

Know the Shell

You can use an IDE (Integrated Development Environment) to code in Ncurses, but I recommend knowing a few shell commands to get the most from a terminal window. It's faster!

THE SHELL PROMPT

The most common shell today is Bash, the Bourne Again Shell. Its default prompt is the dollar sign, which appears as follows in this eBook:

```
$
```

Some terminals may spruce up the prompt with the shell name, your account name, the current directory, and other whatnot. Whatever.

PICK AN EDITOR

If you heed my advice and use the terminal environment, I recommend you use a text-mode editor to create your source code. I'm a fan of *vim*, which is based on *vi* which was written in Curses long ago. Emacs also works, as do various other popular and quirky text editors.

KNOW THY COMPILER

You can compile Ncurses code using the old *cc* compiler, *gcc*, or my favorite, *clang*. You must link in the Ncurses (or Curses) library, as covered later in this chapter.

Ensure that the library and header files are in the proper locations or specify the necessary compiling switches so that the files are located.

USE THE HISTORY COMMAND

Most shells feature a history command. It lets you recall previously-issued commands. You use the history often if you create programs at the command prompt. You can recall the commands to edit, compile, and run your programs quite easily.

In the Bash shell, use the up-arrow key to recall the previous command. You can tap the up-arrow key a few times to continue to recall commands.

THE NCURSES PROJECT FOLDER

I recommend creating an Ncurses directory, in which you can store the exercises and code as you learn.

For example, I place all my programming files in a `prog` directory off my home directory. Ncurses is coded in C (though it can be coded in Python as well), so I place the `ncurses` directory in my `c` directory. Here's the pathname I use:

```
$HOME/prog/c/curses
```

The Ncurses Development Cycle

As with most small coding projects, the process for creating an Ncurses program in this book works in three steps:

1. Write the source code.

2. Compile and link.

3. Run.

If you goof up, and you will, you must repeat this cycle, fixing errors as necessary until the code runs as intended.

Each of these steps can be accomplished at the command prompt quite easily.

If you use an IDE, you'll need to figure out how to create a console or terminal window application. Further, you must cajole the compiler to locate the proper files, including the Ncurses header file and library.

THAT FIRST PROGRAM – SOURCE CODE

Use an editor to create the following code, `01-01_goodbye.c`.

01-01_goodbye.c

```
 1    #include <ncurses.h>
 2
 3    int main()
 4    {
 5        initscr();
 6        addstr(Goodbye, cruel world!);
 7
 8        endwin();
 9        return(0);
10    }
```

At Line 1, the `ncurses.h` header file is included. For most Ncurses projects, that's all you need. If Ncurses is installed in a folder other than the standard `include` folder, ensure that you specify the proper pathname.

Line 5 uses the *initscr()* (initialize screen) function to enter Ncurses, which initializes the screen and creates various data structures.

Line 6 uses the *addstr()* (add string) function to output a line of text to the screen.

Line 8 uses the *endwin()* function to close the Ncurses session.

Beyond the Ncurses functions, the rest of the code is standard C.

THAT FIRST PROGRAM – COMPILING

Here is the command format I use to compile source code, such as the sample code, `01-01_goodbye.c`:

```
clang -lncurses 01-01_goodbye.c
```

The `-l` (lowercase L) switch identifies a library. Above, the `ncurses` library is included – and it's assumed that the library dwells in the same directory as other C language libraries, traditional in `/usr/lib`.

If you receive errors with this format, then specify the library switch last, after the source code filename:

```
clang 01-01_goodbye.c -lncurses
```

Upon success, the default program file `a.out` is created; in Cygwin, the file is named `a.exe`.

When an error occurs, as is deliberately the case here, you see output reflecting the type of errors, warnings, or other information. For *clang*, the following text might be displayed:

```
01-01_goodbye.c:6:18: error: too many arguments provided to
function-like macro invocation
    addstr(Goodbye, cruel world!);

/usr/include/ncurses.h:1016:9: note:
    macro 'addstr' defined here
#define addstr(str)                waddnstr(stdscr,str,-1)
        ^
01-01_goodbye.c:6:2: warning: expression result unused [-
Wunused-value]
        addstr(Goodbye, cruel world!);
```

```
1 warning and 1 error generated.
```

The output is just oozing with information. Key is that problems exist at Line 6 with the *addstr()* function. It requires a string, which isn't enclosed in double-quotes inside the code. It's an easy fix.

THAT FIRST PROGRAM – FIXING THE SOURCE CODE

Programming should really be called *reprogramming*. One of my programmer friends calls it *bugging*. Regardless, fix the code for 01-01_goodbye.c: Change Line 6 to read:

```
6          addstr("Goodbye, cruel world!");
```

♦ *Use the shell's history to recall the previous editing command. Press the up-arrow key twice.*

Save the changes and quit the editor.

THAT FIRST PROGRAM – COMPILING (AGAIN)

Upon compiling you shouldn't see any error messages. If so, check the source code again. Otherwise, run the program:

```
./a.out
```

Or in Cygwin, type:

```
./a
```

And . . . nothing.

Even superficially, you might suspect more to happen. The problem, as is typical with learning any programming language or tool, is that a successful compile and link doesn't always mean that the program does what you intended.

THAT FIRST PROGRAM – FIXING THE CODE (AGAIN)

The code has a central item missing, something that many Ncurses coders forget:

♦ *To display text in Ncurses, you must* refresh *the window.*

Return to the editor and add a new line after Line 6:

```
6+1        refresh();
```

To see the text output by the *addstr()* function, you must refresh the standard screen, Ncurses' primary output window. The *refresh()* function handles that duty.

Save the change.

Compile and run.

The output appears full-screen, though you may not see it. That's because the program runs too quickly and the *endwin()* function closes the Ncurses window before you can blink.

One more fix: Insert a new Line 8:

```
8  |            getch();
```

The *getch()* function waits to fetch a character from the keyboard. It works like pause key, allowing you to see the program on the screen, then press "any key" to quit.

Because the code has been altered sufficiently, here is the full listing for 01-01_goodbye.c:

01-02_goodbye-final.c

```
1   #include <ncurses.h>
2
3   int main(void)
4   {
5           initscr();
6           addstr("Goodbye, cruel C programming!");
7           refresh();
8           getch();
9
10          endwin();
11          return(0);
12  }
```

6

2. Basic Input/Output

As a text screen library, Ncurses deals primarily with input and output, the old I/O you sang about at computer camp. If you're familiar with stream I/O in C, Ncurses lets you control the terminal in a more interactive manner – a method used by most full-screen programs.

The Ncurses Skeleton

All Ncurses programs have the same basic skeleton, which looks something like this:

02-01_skeleton.c

```
 1    #include <ncurses.h>
 2
 3    int main()
 4    {
 5        initscr();   /* Initialize Ncurses */
 6
 7        /* other programming */
 8
 9        endwin();    /* close Ncurses */
10        return(0);
11    }
```

The ncurses.h header file defines the functions and constants you use to access the Ncurses library.

The bookend functions are *initscr()* and *endwin()*. One activates Ncurses, the other closes the session.

Once activated, you can use Ncurses functions to control the screen. The screen clears and your program does whatever wondrous thing it does.

The *endwin()* function terminates the Ncurses session, but it does not quit your program. You must do that yourself, such as the simple *return* shown in the skeleton sample.

THE NCURSES HEADER FILE

The ncurses.h header file defines various constants and function prototypes. It's required.

♦ *The header file is not the same as the Ncurses library. The library is linked in after you compile the code.*

The Ncurses header file does a few nifty tricks. First, it automatically includes the following header files:

`stdio.h`

`unctrl.h`

`stdarg.h`

`stddef.h`

Therefore, you don't need to redundantly include these header files in your source code.

Also, the `ncurses.h` file defines useful constants such as TRUE, FALSE, OK, ERR, and others.

THE *INITSCR()* FUNCTION

The *initscr()* function initializes Ncurses. It does not clear the terminal screen. Instead it sets up internal memory structures and interfaces between the Ncurses functions and the terminal window's I/O system.

Two important items the *initscr()* function creates are called the *standard screen* and the *current screen*. Both are used by Ncurses to splash information up on the terminal screen.

THE STANDARD SCREEN

The standard screen is the default output window for Ncurses. All Ncurses output commands, plus a select few input commands, are window-oriented. The standard screen is the main window, and it's the same size as the terminal screen. The *initscr()* function creates the standard screen and uses the variable `stdscr` to reference it.

THE CURRENT SCREEN

The standard screen is not the same as the terminal window, and stuff you write to the standard screen doesn't immediately appear on the terminal window. To update the terminal window, the standard screen must be refreshed.

To monitor the difference between what's displayed (or what Ncurses assumes is displayed) and the standard screen, an internal buffer called the *current screen* is used.

♦   *The current screen is referenced by using the variable* `curscr`.

What the *refresh()* function does is to update text on the current screen to match the standard screen. In fact, only differences between the two buffers are updated.

When a disconnect occurs between the standard screen and current screen, you can "touch" the standard screen to update its entire contents. This process is covered later in this eBook.

The screen-writing process is done in multiple steps to keep text output efficient. The other way would be to update the complete terminal screen each time new text is output, which can be maddeningly slow or may cause the terminal to flicker.

STEPPING THROUGH AN EXAMPLE

As a review, Chapter 1 introduced the `01-01_goodbye.c` source code. Here's the final version of that code:

01-02_goodbye-final.c

```
 1     #include  <ncurses.h>
 2
 3     int main()
 4     {
 5          initscr();
 6          addstr("Goodbye, cruel world!");
 7          refresh();
 8          getch();
 9
10          endwin();
11          return(0);
12     }
```

In Line 5 the *initscr()* function configures Ncurses and creates both the standard screen and current screen. It also clears the current terminal window. If the terminal uses the *rmcup* feature, then the screen is saved and then restored after the Ncurses program exits. (*rmcup* is a terminal attribute.)

In Line 6, the *addstr()* function writes a string to the standard screen. The `stdscr` variable need not be specified, as the *addstr()* function (actually, a macro) outputs to the standard screen by default.

At this point in the code, nothing appears on the screen.

The *refresh()* function at Line 7 updates the virtual screen, which immediately updates the current screen. For the user, the text appears in the terminal window.

In Line 8, the program pauses while the *getch()* function awaits keyboard input. Unlike the *getchar()* function (standard C I/O), the user doesn't have to press the Enter key; *getch()* immediately reads any non-shift key.

The *endwin()* function shuts down Ncurses in Line 10. If the terminal supports *rmcup*, the original screen is restored at this point.

Line 11 returns control back to the shell.

♦   *It's very important that you use the* endwin() *function to finish your Ncurses code!*

If you neglect to use *endwin()*, the terminal's behavior becomes unpredictable.

STANDARD C I/O UNDER NCURSES

Keep in mind that the standard C output functions — *putc()*, *puts()*, *printf()*, and so on — work while Ncurses is active. You don't see their output, however, until the *endwin()* function is called.

Don't fret if you think you're missing a favorite input or output function. Ncurses sports counterparts for each standard C I/O function, as covered in the next section.

Text Output

Three common Ncurses text-output functions are *addch()*, *addstr()*, and *printw()*. These functions are similar to the standard C library functions, *putchar()*, *puts()*, and *printf()*:

```
addch(ch)
```

```
addstr(*string)
```

```
printw(format,arg...)
```

The *addch()* function places (adds) a single character to the screen, similar to the *putchar()* function.

The *addstr()* function adds an entire string to the screen, similar to calling *addch()* over and over. Unlike the *puts()* function, a newline (\n) isn't appended to output.

The *printw()* function is the Ncurses version of *printf()*. It uses the standard *printf()* placeholders and variables to output formatted text.

Additional text output functions, as well as variations on these three, are available in the Ncurses library.

ONE CHARACTER AT A TIME

I love marquee programs. Rather than write a really fancy one, which Ncurses is more than capable of doing, the following code, 02-02_add1.c uses the *addch()* function to output a single character and the *napms()* function to set a delay.

02-02_add1.c

```
1    #include  <ncurses.h>
2
3    int main()
4    {
5         char text[] = "Greetings from Ncurses!";
6         char *t;
7
8         initscr();              /* initialize Ncurses */
9         t = text;               /* initialize the pointer */
10
11        while(*t)               /* loop through the string */
12        {
13             addch(*t);         /* one char output */
14             t++;               /* increment the pointer */
15             refresh();         /* update the screen */
16             napms(100);        /* delay .1 sec */
17        }
18        getch();                /* wait here */
19
20        endwin();               /* clean up Ncurses */
21        return(0);
22    }
```

This code uses a pointer t to inch through a string of text. Along the way, the *addch()* function outputs the character (Line 13).

At Line 16, the *napms()* function pauses output one tenth of a second between each character displayed. Think "nap for milliseconds," with the millisecond value as the *napms()* function's argument. So napms(1000) pauses output for one second.

The position of the *refresh()* function is important in this code! It appears at Line 15, which causes each character output to be displayed one at a time. If you edit the code and place the

11

refresh() after the *while* loop, you see the text all at once, which isn't the intended outcome.

A FULL STRING

The *addstr()* function displays a full string of text. Its argument is a string variable (*char* array), constant, or immediate value. A newline is not appended to the output.

02-03_add2.c

```
1    #include <ncurses.h>
2
3    int main()
4    {
5            char t1[] = "Shall I compare thee";
6            char t2[] = " to a summer's day?";
7
8            initscr();
9            addstr(t1);      /* add the first string */
10           addstr(t2);      /* add the second string */
11           refresh();       /* display the result */
12           getch();         /* wait */
13
14           endwin();
15           return(0);
16   }
```

The *addstr()* function's argument doesn't appear until the next *refresh()* function updates the screen.

The effect of the two *addstr()* functions is to display the text on a single line:

```
Shall I compare thee to a summer's day?
```

Afterwards, the cursor rests at the end of the line. If string t2 had a newline (\n) at the end, the cursor would be at the start of the next line, as would also be the case with standard output.

OUTPUT LOCATION

Cursor behavior in Ncurses mimics behavior of standard output. A long line of text wraps around at the end of a terminal screen row (far right column) and continues on the next line. A newline moves the cursor to the start of the next line.

Ncurses offers more control than standard output. For example, the cursor's position can be relocated at any time. The following code uses the *move()* function to change cursor location.

02-04_add3.c

```
1     #include <ncurses.h>
2
3     int main()
4     {
5         char t1[] = "Shall I compare thee";
6         char t2[] = " to a summer's day?";
7
8         initscr();
9         addstr(t1);      /* add the first string */
10        addstr(t2);      /* add the second string */
11        move(2,0);       /* row 3, column 1 */
12        addstr("Though art more lovely...");
13        refresh();       /* display the result */
14        getch();         /* wait */
15
16        endwin();
17        return(0);
18    }
```

The *move()* function in Line 11 relocates the cursor to the third row, first column. As with array elements and other C counting, the first column and row on the screen are numbered zero; position 2,0 is the third row, first column. The output looks like this:

```
Shall I compare thee to a summer's day?

Though art more lovely...
```

After the cursor has moved, Line 12 uses the *addstr()* function to place another line of text at the new position.

Here is the format of the *move()* function:

move(y,x)

y is a row value, with zero as the top (first) row on the standard screen up to as many rows as are available.

x is a column value, starting with zero at the far-left column and incrementing until the far-right position for the current screen size.

♦ *It's important to remember that the* move() *function's arguments have the row first, or Y, X (if you're familiar with Cartesian coordinates). Think "row, column" as opposed to X, Y.*

FORMATTED TEXT OUTPUT

The Ncurses *printw()* function is the counterpart to the standard C library's *printf()* function. Use it to display strings of text,

13

variables, formatted text, and all that stuff. If you know *printf()*, then you also know *printw()*.

02-05_yoda.c

```
1     #include <ncurses.h>
2
3     int main()
4     {
5             int yoda = 874;
6             int ss = 65;
7
8             initscr();
9             printw("Yoda is %d years old\n",yoda);
10            printw("He has collected %d years",yoda-ss);
11            printw(" of Social Security.");
12            refresh();
13            getch();
14
15     endwin();
16     return(0);
17     }
```

This code runs the same as you would expect had *printf()* been used, though the output is full-screen.

Text Input

Ncurses doesn't use an input stream. Characters can be checked, fetched as they come in, linger in a queue, and so on. This type of behavior is natural if you've used text mode programs, but it differs greatly from the standard C library input functions.

Popular Ncurses console input functions include *getch()*, which you've seen in most of the samples so far, and *getstr()*, *getnstr()*, and *scanw()*.

```
getch()
```

```
getstr(*buf)
```

```
getnstr(*buf,n)
```

```
scanw(format,*var)
```

The *getch()* function returns a single character from the console. The user doesn't need to press the Enter key, the character is fetched immediately. If no character is available, execution waits.

The *getstr()* and *getnstr()* functions read a string of text. Of the two, use *getnstr()*, which measures input and is more secure.

The *scanw()* function works just like the standard I/O function *scanf()*. It allows for formatted input.

Ncurses input functions aren't limited to these four. Additional functions let you massage input and read special keys.

A SILLY TYPEWRITER PROGRAM

Nothing best demonstrates "one character in/one character out" than a simple, stupid typewriter program, such as the one below.

02-06_typewriter.c

```
1    #include <ncurses.h>
2
3    int main()
4    {
5        int ch;
6
7        initscr();
8        addstr("Type a few lines of text\n");
9        addstr("Press ~ to quit\n");
10       refresh();
11
12       while( (ch = getch()) != '~')
13           ;
14
15       endwin();
16       return(0);
17   }
```

The meat of the code is the *while* loop at Line 12. It uses the *getch()* function to read input and store it in variable ch. If that character isn't the ~ (tilde), the loop repeats.

Variable ch can be an *int* or a *char*. The *getch()* function is defined as generating integer output, though *char* variables work in most circumstances.

A single-character output function isn't required because *getch()* echoes text input by default. You can disable this effect, which is covered later in this eBook.

♦ *In this code's program, you might see that pressing the Enter key generates a carriage return but no linefeed. This is a function of the terminal, not of Ncurses.*

A WHOLE STRING OF TEXT

The Ncurses *getstr()* function works similar to the standard *gets()* function. As with *gets()*, I don't recommend that you use *getstr()* as it offers no input-bounds checking: It's possible to overflow the buffer, which is a security risk. Therefore, I recommend that you instead use the *getnstr()* function, which provides a limit to the amount of text input, as shown in the following code.

02-07_yourname.c

```
 1    #include <ncurses.h>
 2
 3    int main()
 4    {
 5            char first[24];
 6            char last[32];
 7
 8            initscr();
 9            addstr("What is your first name? ");
10            refresh();
11            getnstr(first,23);
12
13            addstr("What is your last name? ");
14            refresh();
15            getnstr(last,31);
16
17            printw("Pleased to meet you, %s %s!",first,last);
18            refresh();
19            getch();
20
21            endwin();
22            return(0);
23    }
```

Only 24 characters are allocated for *char* buffer `first` (Line 5). And 32 characters are allocated for *char* buffer `last` (Line 6).

The *getnstring()* function at Line 11 reads up to 23 characters from the keyboard. If the user types more, a beep sounds. The 23 characters doesn't include the null character (\0) at the end of the string, which is why the value read is one less than the buffer size.

The *refresh()* functions after the *addstr()* functions (Lines 10 and 14) ensure that the prompts appear on the screen. Likewise, a *refresh()* is required at line 18 to ensure that the *printw()* function's output appears.

Here is a sample run:

```
What is your first name? Clark
What is your last name? Kent
Pleased to meet you, Clark Kent!
```

Users can backspace and erase after hitting the maximum number of characters that *getnstr()* allows; they cannot type

more. So unlike stream-input functions, such as *fgets()*, any text
that flows in after the maximum is lost.

THE OBLIGATORY *SCANW( )* PROGRAM

I'm not a big *scanf()* fan (as you know if you've read my C
programming books), therefore you're not going to be seeing
much of *scanw()* in this book. Given that, here is the obligatory
demonstration of *scanw()*, which works similar to *scanf()* in the
standard C library:

02_08_sushi.c

```
1    #include <ncurses.h>
2
3    int main()
4    {
5         int pieces;
6         const float uni = 4.5;
7
8         initscr();
9
10        addstr("SUSHI BAR");
11        move(2,0);
12        printw("We have Uni today for $%.2f.\n",uni);
13        addstr("How many pieces would you like? ");
14        refresh();
15
16        scanw("%d",&pieces);
17        printw("You want %d pieces?\n",pieces);
18        printw("That will be $%.2f!",uni*(float)pieces);
19        refresh();
20        getch();
21
22        endwin();
23        return(0);
25    }
```

The *scanw()* function works just like *scanf()*. In Line 16, it reads an
integer value from input and stores it in variable `pieces`.

♦ *As with* scanf(), *don't forget the address-of operator (*&*) when using a
non-pointer variable with* scanw().

3. Formatting Text

Ncurses text styles may not be as elaborate as the styles offered in a GUI word processor, but they're enough to add emphasis, fun, and perhaps a wee bit o' color to what would otherwise be boring terminal text.

Text Abuse with Text Attributes

Ncurses has three functions to control the tone of the text displayed on the screen: *attrset()*, *attron()*, and *attroff()*. The *attr* part of the function name is short for *attribute*.

```
attrset(attrs)
```

```
attron(attrs)
```

```
attroff(attrs)
```

The *attrset()* function directs Ncurses to apply the named attribute(s), `attrs`, to all text displayed from that point onward.

The *attron()* and *attroff()* functions turn specific text attributes on or off, respectively.

You can use either *attrset()* or *attorn()* to initially apply text attributes.

```
attrset(A_BOLD);
```

```
attron(A_BOLD);
```

Both the above statements apply the bold text (`A_BOLD`) attribute to any text displayed afterward. The difference is that *attrset()* turns off all other attributes previously applied, leaving only bold applied to the text, where *attron()* adds the bold attribute to any attributes already applied to the text.

♦ *Text attributes affect only text, not the whitespace between words.*

TEXT ATTRIBUTE ROUNDUP

Without specifying otherwise, Ncurses uses the normal (`A_NORMAL`) text attribute. That equates to the standard white text on a black background, or however you have your terminal configured, such as green text on a white background, whatever.

Table 3-1 lists the basic (non-color) text attributes you can apply to text. These are valid arguments for the *attrset()*, *attron()*, and *attroff()* functions.

ATTRIBUTE NAME	WHAT IT DOES
A_ALTCHARSET	Displays text using an alternative character set (defined by your terminal)
A_BLINK	Damned blinking text (which may be disabled for your terminal)
A_BOLD	Bright text
A_DIM	Dimmed text (not as bright as regular text)
A_INVIS	Hidden text
A_NORMAL	Normal text
A_REVERSE	Black-on-white text
A_STANDOUT	Generate a "standout" attribute, usually inverse text
A_UNDERLINE	Underline text
A_PROTECT	Protected text, available only on certain terminals, prevents text from being over-written
A_HORIZONTAL A_LEFT A_LOW A_RIGHT A_TOP A_VERTICAL	Not implemented. My guess is that these attributes set text direction or orientation

Table 3-1. Ncurses text attributes.

SET AND RESET ATTRIBUTES

The following code runs through the various text attributes, demonstrating how they can be applied.

03-01_twinkle.c

```
1    #include <ncurses.h>
2
3    int main()
4    {
5            initscr();
6
7            attron(A_BOLD);
8            addstr("Twinkle, twinkle little star\n");
9            attron(A_BLINK);
10           addstr("How I wonder what you are.\n");
11           attroff(A_BOLD);
12           addstr("Up above the world so high,\n");
13           addstr("Like a diamond in the sky.\n");
14           attrset(A_NORMAL);
15           addstr("Twinkle, twinkle little star\n");
16           addstr("How I wonder what you are.\n");
17           refresh();
18           getch();
19
20           endwin();
21           return(0);
22   }
```

An attribute stays on until you turn it off, either via *attroff()* or *attrset()*. Otherwise the attributes are slapped on to all text output after the attribute function is used.

MULTIPLE ATTRIBUTES

You don't have to issue multiple *attrset()*, *attron()*, or *attroff()* functions to apply or remove multiple attributes. Because each attribute has a unique bit pattern, you can combine them in a single statement by using a logical OR operator between them.

For example, if you want your text bold and blinking, you can use:

```
attrset(A_BOLD | A_BLINK);
```

Above, both the bold and blink attributes are specified, meaning any text displayed after that statement will boldly blink (highly irritating).

03-02_annoy.c

```
1    #include <ncurses.h>
2
3    #define COUNT 5
4
5    int main()
6    {
7            char text[COUNT][10] = {
```

```
 8                    "Do", "you", "find", "this", "silly?"
 9             };
10             int a,b;
11
12             initscr();
13
14             for(a=0;a<COUNT;a++)
15             {
16                     for(b=0;b<COUNT;b++)
17                     {
18                             if(b==a) attrset(A_BOLD | A_UNDERLINE);
19                             printw("%s",text[b]);
20                             if(b==a) attroff(A_BOLD | A_UNDERLINE);
21                             addch(' ');
22                     }
23                     addstr("\b\n");
24             }
25             refresh();
26             getch();
27
28             endwin();
29             return(0);
30     }
```

THE *STANDEND()* FUNCTION

Another way to turn off all attributes is to use the *standend()* function:

```
standend()
```

This function is defined in the `ncurses.h` header file as a macro for the `attrset(A_NORMAL)` statement, which resets all text output back to normal text.

Can It Do Color?

Ncurses can do color, but can your terminal? Don't bother searching for an answer, just use the *has_colors()* function:

```
has_colors()
```

The statement returns a logical TRUE if the terminal can display colored text, FALSE otherwise.

When *has_colors()* returns TRUE, use the *start_color()* function to initialize color capabilities:

```
start_color()
```

The *start_color()* function returns OK to indicate that color functions are properly initialized. Once confirmed, you define

22

color pairs, which are then applied to text in the same manner as text attributes.

♦ *TRUE, FALSE, and OK are defined in the* **ncurses.h** *header file.*

The following code determines whether the terminal window can do colors. It reports how many colors and color combinations are available for the color pairs, or attributes, which can be used in your code.

03-03_colortest.c

```
 1   #include <ncurses.h>
 2
 3   int main()
 4   {
 5           initscr();
 6
 7   /* test for color ability of the terminal */
 8           if(!has_colors())
 9           {
10                   endwin();                   /* exit Ncurses */
11                   puts("Terminal cannot do colors");
12                   return(1);
13           }
14
15   /* initialize Ncurses colors */
16           if(start_color() != OK)
17           {
18                   endwin();
19                   puts("Unable to start colors.");
20                   return(1);
21           }
22
23   /* colors are okay; continue */
24           printw("Colors initialized.\n");
25           printw("%d colors available.\n",COLORS);
26           printw("%d color pairs.",COLOR_PAIRS);
27           refresh();
28           getch();
29
30           endwin();
31           return(0);
32   }
```

Here's the output I see on my computer:

```
Colors initialized.
8 colors available.
64 color pairs.
```

The COLORS and COLOR_PAIRS constants are set when the *start_color()* function determines how many colors are available for the terminal. Also coming into play is how much space is left for storing color information in the Ncurses *attr_t* variable type.

COLORS AND COLOR PAIRS

Ncurses uses the COLORS and COLOR_PAIRS constants to report how many colors the terminal can display and how many color combinations can be defined.

The COLORS value reflects the basic set of colors available. A typical terminal reports only eight colors, which are the standard text colors used on PCs since way back when. The colors are listed in Table 3-2, along with their Ncurses constant names and values.

NCURSES NUMBER	PC BIOS NUMBER	HUE	PC NAME	NCURSES NAME
0	0		Black	COLOR_BLACK
1	4		Red	COLOR_RED
2	2		Green	COLOR_GREEN
3	6		Brown	COLOR_YELLOW
4	1		Blue	COLOR_BLUE
5	5		Magenta	COLOR_MAGENTA
6	3		Cyan	COLOR_CYAN
7	7		White	COLOR_WHITE

Table 3-2: Ncurses colors.

It's important to remember that the COLORS value tells you how many colors are available, yet the color numbers start with zero. So, the range is 0 through COLORS-1.

A color pair is a combination of foreground and background color attributes. Each color pair is assigned a number from 1 through the value of COLOR_PAIRS.

For example, the color pair COLOR_YELLOW, COLOR_RED indicates yellow text on a red background. To assign those colors as a text attribute you first use the *init_pair()* function:

```
init_pair(n,foreground,background)
```

Argument n is the color pair number; foreground and background are the Ncurses names for the colors.

```
init_pair(1,COLOR_YELLOW,COLOR_RED);
```

The above statement defines color pair number 1 as yellow text on a red background.

Once defined, color pairs use the *attrset()* or *attron()* function to apply color to text. The attribute is COLOR_PAIR(n), where n matches the defined color pair value.

```
attrset(COLOR_PAIR(1));
```

Above, color pair 1 is set for the text that follows. If COLOR_PAIR(1) is defined as yellow text on a red background, that's the attribute assigned to the text.

The following code displays a line of yellow text on a red background.

03-04_yellowred.c

```
1   #include <ncurses.h>
2
3   int main()
4   {
5       initscr();
6       start_color();
7       init_pair(1,COLOR_YELLOW,COLOR_RED);
8       addstr("Normal text\n");
9       attrset(COLOR_PAIR(1));
10      addstr("Colored text. Wee!\n");
11      attrset(A_NORMAL);
12      addstr("Back to normal.");
13      refresh();
14      getch();
15
16      endwin();
17      return(0);
18  }
```

The *start_color()* function at Line 6 initializes color capabilities. Unlike the preceding sample code, I'm not verifying that the terminal is color-capable. (This omission is to keep the sample code short, as I wrote in the Introduction.)

Color pair 1 is assigned in Line 7: yellow text on a red background.

In Line 9, the COLOR_PAIR(1) attribute is set, applied to all text displayed afterwards, which is primarily Line 10.

In Line 11, normal text attributes are restored.

EIGHT OR SIXTEEN COLORS?

On most terminals, Ncurses specifies that only 8 colors available, the value of the COLORS constant. In fact, you'll find twice that number too choose from. The secret is to apply the bold text attribute (A_BOLD) with a color pair.

The bold text attribute augments the foreground text color, giving you access to brighter versions of the standard text colors. For a terminal with 8 colors available, adding the A_BOLD attribute gives you 16 possible foreground colors.

The following code creates a second color pair. Text with both color pair attributes is displayed, then displayed again along with the A_BOLD attribute:

03-05_colorful.c

```
1    #include <ncurses.h>
2
3    int main()
4    {
5        initscr();
6        start_color();
7        init_pair(1,COLOR_BLACK,COLOR_RED);
8        init_pair(2,COLOR_YELLOW,COLOR_BLACK);
9        attrset(COLOR_PAIR(1));         /* black on red */
10       addstr("I am Mr. Black!\n");
11       attrset(COLOR_PAIR(2));         /* yellow on black */
12       addstr("I am Mr. Yellow!\n");
13       attrset(COLOR_PAIR(1) | A_BOLD);      /* +bold */
14       addstr("I'm feeling bold!\n");
15       attrset(COLOR_PAIR(2) | A_BOLD);;     /* +bold */
16       addstr("Me too!");
17       refresh();
18       getch();
19
20       endwin();
21       return(0);
22   }
```

Each time the *attrset()* function is used (Lines 9, 11, 13, and 15), a new attribute is applied (not replaced). In Lines 13 and 15, the A_BOLD attribute is mixed in with the original color pairs. The effect may be profound on some terminals, or just bold text.

♦ *Color pair attributes affect only the text put to the screen. The red background doesn't fill the rest of the line. The foreground color, like other text attributes, affects only characters and not the blanks or white space between text.*

A COLOR THING YOUR TERMINAL PROBABLY CANNOT DO

Not every terminal can spin up a palette of text colors. The way to find out is to use the *can_change_color()* function:

```
can_change_color()
```

The function returns a logical **TRUE** or **FALSE** depending on the terminal's capabilities. If s **TRUE**, you can use the *init_color()* function to build a custom color:

```
init_color(n,red,green,blue)
```

Argument n represents the new color number. It must be in the range of zero to **COLOR-1**. The next three arguments represent values of the additive colors red, green, and blue (respectively), with values ranging from 0 to 1000.

```
init_color(1,1000,750,750);
```

Above, new color 1 is created. It's composed of 100 percent red, 75 percent green, and 75 percent blue hues. That works out to pink.

03-06_pink.c

```
1    #include <ncurses.h>
2
3    #define PINK 1
4
5    int main()
6    {
7            initscr();
8
9            start_color();
10           if(!can_change_color())
11                   addstr("This probably won't work...\n");
12
13           init_color(PINK,1000,750,750);      /* pink */
14           init_pair(1,PINK,COLOR_BLACK);
15           attrset(COLOR_PAIR(1));
16           printw("This is the new color %d.\n",PINK);
17           refresh();
18           getch();
19
20           endwin();
21           return(0);
22   }
```

Line 3 defines a constant **PINK** set to number 1. You don't have to do this, though I wanted to track the new color by using that constant instead of just the value 1.

Line 10 tests the *can_change_color()* function. If **FALSE** is returned, a message is displayed. Otherwise, no harm is done to attempt to create a new color

In Line 13, the *init_color()* function assigns a new color value to constant **PINK**, which is color 1 (originally red). If the *can_change_color()* function fails, then a new color isn't assigned, and color 1 remains red.

Color a Window

Colors in Ncurses can be both text attributes as well as screen or window attributes. To set the standard screen background color, use the *bkgd()* function:

```
bkgd(attrs)
```

This function works similarly to the *attrset()* function for text: You first create a color pair, then assign that color pair to the standard screen (or window). For example:

```
bkgd(COLOR_PAIR(1));
```

The foreground and background colors assigned to `COLOR_PAIR(1)` are applied to the standard screen – the entire window. All text displayed inherits the screen background color, though you can use *attrset()* and *attorn()* functions to spot-change text color or other attributes.

SCREEN BACKGROUND COLOR

The following code colors the standard screen blue:

03-07_bgcolor1.c

```
1    #include <ncurses.h>
2
3    int main()
4    {
5            initscr();
6
7            start_color();
8            init_pair(1,COLOR_WHITE,COLOR_BLUE);
9            bkgd(COLOR_PAIR(1));
10           refresh();
11           getch();
12
13           endwin();
14           return(0);
15   }
```

The code also colors text white, though because no text is displayed, you see only blue.

To add some text, insert the following after Line 9:

```
9+1              addstr("This is some text");
```

The text appears white on a blue background.

MORE THAN SOLID

The *bkgd()* function sets any text attribute to the entire screen. That's because the argument to the *bkgd()* function is a _chtype_ _character_. This special, Ncurses variable includes both text character and attribute information. Therefore, you can specify a single character as the background attribute for a window.

```
bkgd('.');
```

The above statement fills the window's background with periods. They appear between words as well because it's the dot that defines the window's text background attribute.

To combine a character with an attribute, use the logical OR operator, as in:

```
bkgd(COLOR_PAIR(1)   | '.');
```

The | (logical OR) takes the value of COLOR_PAIR(1) and combines it with the character code for a period (`.`). The result is a screen filled with white dots on a blue background.

CHANGE COLOR ON-THE-FLY

The *bkgd()* function can be applied at any time without affecting any text already on the window. The function only alters attributes.

03-08_bgcolor2.c

```
1     #include <ncurses.h>
2
3     int main()
4     {
5             initscr();
6
7             start_color();
8             init_pair(1,COLOR_WHITE,COLOR_BLUE);
9             init_pair(2,COLOR_GREEN,COLOR_WHITE);
10            init_pair(3,COLOR_RED,COLOR_GREEN);
11            bkgd(COLOR_PAIR(1));
12
13            addstr("I think that I shall never see\n");
```

```
14              addstr("a color screen as pretty as thee.\n");
15              addstr("For seasons may change\n");
16              addstr("and storms may thunder;\n");
17              addstr("But color text shall always wonder.");
18              refresh();
19              getch();
20
21              bkgd(COLOR_PAIR(2));
22              refresh();
23              getch();
24
25              bkgd(COLOR_PAIR(3));
26              refresh();
27              getch();
28
29              endwin();
30              return(0);
31      }
```

The program initially displays some text on the screen, blue on a white background. Press the Enter key and the colors change to green on a white background; the text is unchanged. Press Enter again and the text color changes to red, the background to green. Ugly.

Noise, too!

Computer terminals traditionally sport some method of getting attention. The early teletypes featured a bell, which is still ASCII code 7 (^G). Terminal windows in GUI operating systems also feature a beep or some alert technique. To implement these features, Ncurses offers the *beep()* and *flash()* functions.

```
beep()
```

```
flash()
```

The *beep()* function, as you can guess, beeps the terminal's speaker or generates whatever tone is assigned to the terminal window program.

The *flash()* function gets attention by flashing the screen. This function assists the hearing impaired to recognize alerts. Sadly, it's not implemented on every terminal, so the function may just beep the speaker

03-09_notice.c

```
1       #include <ncurses.h>
2
3       int main()
```

```
4        {
5              initscr();
6
7              addstr("Attention!\n");
8              beep();
9              refresh();
10             getch();
11
12             addstr("I said, ATTENTION!\n");
13             flash();
14             refresh();
15             getch();
16
17             endwin();
18             return(0);
19        }
```

After you see **Attention!** on the screen, you hear the beep.
Press Enter to see **I said, ATTENTION!** and look for the flash.
On my computer, I just heard another beep.

4. More Than a Character

A *chtype* is a special variable that holds a combination of character and attribute information. It's 32-bits wide, typically the size of an *int* or *long int*, depending on the system. That's wider than a *char* variable, which is usually 8-bits wide.

The 32-bits of the *chtype* are packed with character and attribute information. When you use a *chtype* variable, you can apply text, color, and other attributes all at once. This data stays with the character, even when you use Ncurses functions to copy the text.

Nothing special is required to use *chtype* characters. All character positions on the screen or window are *chtype*. Further, you don't have to specify the full *chtype* for each character you put to the screen.

Attributes and *chtype* Characters

The *chtype* character arguments are used with most Ncurses text-output functions, such as *addch()*. When you specify a *chtype* variable as the function's argument, you don't need to bother with the *attorn()*, *attrset()*, and *attroff()* functions to set attributes; just put the *chtype* to the screen.

PUT TEXT AND ATTRIBUTES ON THE SCREEN

The common way to build a *chtype* is to use the bitwise OR operator, |, to combine a character and attribute. For example:

```
addch('E' | A_BOLD);
```

Order isn't important; you can specify the attribute first:

```
addch(A_BOLD | 'E');
```

The above function displays the character E with the bold attribute at the cursor's current position.

04-01_charattrib.c

```
1    #include <ncurses.h>
2
3    int main()
4    {
5        initscr();
6
```

```
 7              addch('c');
 8              addch(A_BOLD | 'a');
 9              addch(A_REVERSE | 't');
10              refresh();
11              getch();
12
13              endwin();
14              return(0);
15      }
```

The three *addch()* functions are Lines 7, 8, and 9 put *chtype* characters to the standard screen. The output looks like this:

`cat`

(The a above is in boldface.)

UPDATE TEXT

When a *chtype* character is used with an output function, such as *addch()*, any attributes previously applied to a character position are overwritten. The following code updates 04-01_charattrib.c, replacing the t in *cat* with an r:

04-02_changechar.c

```
 1      #include <ncurses.h>
 2
 3      int main()
 4      {
 5              initscr();
 6
 7              addch('c');
 8              addch(A_BOLD | 'a');
 9              addch(A_REVERSE | 't');
10              refresh();
11              getch();
12
13              /* replace the 't' with 'r' */
14              move(0,2);
15              addch('r');
16              refresh();
17              getch();
18
19              endwin();
20              return(0);
21      }
```

Because the *addch()* function in Line 15 doesn't specify any attributes, only character 'r' is placed on the screen, over-writing the 't' and its attributes.

If you want to retain the attributes, you must apply the proper *chtype*, as in:

```
addch(A_REVERSE | 'r');
```

TEXT ATTRIBUTE ROUNDUP

Internally, the *chtype* variable represents 32-bits of data as follows:

- Bits 0 to 7 are the character code (ASCII)

- Bits 8 to 15 contain color values.

- Bits 16 to 31 represent the individual attributes.

Table 4-1 lists the individual attributes available for bits 16 through 31. Not every terminal supports all the attributes.

ATTRIBUTE NAME	DESCRIPTION	BIT POSITION	HEX MASK
A_STANDOUT	Highlight the text so that it stands out	16	0x00010000
A_UNDERLINE	Underline text	17	0x00020000
A_REVERSE	Text foreground and background colors are reversed	18	0x00040000
A_BLINK	Text blinks	19	0x00080000
A_DIM	Text is dimmed	20	0x00100000
A_BOLD	Text is bold (intense)	21	0x00200000
A_ALTCHARSET	Activate the alternative character set	22	0x00400000
A_INVIS	Text is invisible	23	0x00800000
A_PROTECT	Text is protected	24	0x01000000
A_HORIZONTAL	Text is displayed horizontally	25	0x02000000

A_LEFT	Text is displayed on the left	26	0x04000000
A_LOW	Text is displayed low	27	0x08000000
A_RIGHT	Text is displayed on the right	28	0x10000000
A_TOP	Text is displayed high (top)	29	0x20000000
A_VERTICAL	Text is displayed vertically	30	0x40000000
Unused	Unused	31	0x80000000

Table 4-1. Text attribute bit positions.

The first several attributes listed in Table 4-1 are what I refer to as traditional text attributes, modifying the way characters appear.

Using the A_ALTCHARSET attribute is covered in the next section.

The A_INVIS attribute allows text to be present on the screen, yet invisible. The A_PROTECT prevents text from being altered. Implementation of these attributes isn't available on every terminal.

The final attributes deal with text orientation and direction. As you may suspect, not every terminal supports these attributes.

The following code demonstrates each attribute, though I use the *attrset()* command and not *chtype* variables directly. Even so, because attributes and characters are combined on the screen, result is the same as if *chtype* characters were punched to various positions on the screen.

04-03_attrtest.c

```
1    #include <ncurses.h>
2
3    int main()
4    {
5        initscr();
6
7        attrset(A_STANDOUT);
8        addstr("This is A_STANDOUT\n");
9        attrset(A_UNDERLINE);
```

```
10        addstr("This is A_UNDERLINE\n");
11        attrset(A_REVERSE);
12        addstr("This is A_REVERSE\n");
13        attrset(A_BLINK);
14        addstr("This is A_BLINK\n");
15        attrset(A_DIM);
16        addstr("This is A_DIM\n");
17        attrset(A_BOLD);
18        addstr("This is A_BOLD\n");
19        attrset(A_ALTCHARSET);
20        addstr("This is A_ALTCHARSET\n");
21        attrset(A_INVIS);
22        addstr("This is A_INVIS\n");
23        attrset(A_PROTECT);
42        addstr("This is A_PROTECT\n");
25        attrset(A_HORIZONTAL);
26        addstr("This is A_HORIZONTAL\n");
27        attrset(A_LEFT);
28        addstr("This is A_LEFT\n");
29        attrset(A_LOW);
30        addstr("This is A_LOW\n");
31        attrset(A_RIGHT);
32        addstr("This is A_RIGHT\n");
33        attrset(A_TOP);
34        addstr("This is A_TOP\n");
35        attrset(A_VERTICAL);
36        addstr("This is A_VERTICAL\n");
37
38        refresh();
39        getch();
40
41        endwin();
42        return(0);
43     }
```

The output you see on the terminal depends on which attributes it supports.

You can apply a masking constant to further manipulate *chtype* variables. These constants are defined in the ncurses.h header file and shown in Table 4-2.

ATTRIBUTE NAME	MASKS	VALUE (HEX)
A_NORMAL	Nothing	0x00000000
A_ATTRIBUTES	Attributes only	0xFFFFFF00
A_CHARTEXT	Character only	0x000000FF
A_COLOR	Color info only	0x0000FF00

Table 4-2. Text attribute masking values.

♦ *I recommend using the attribute name and not its value.*

Another set of attributes is available, one that adheres to the XSI standard. These attributes use the same suffix as those shown in Tables 4-1 and 4-2, though the prefix WA_ is used instead of A_.

The Alternative Character Set

Beyond the standard ASCII characters, Ncurses provides access to the alternative character set, or ACS. Many of these characters are defined as constants in the ncurses.h header file, and they're accessed by using the A_ALTCHARSET attribute in the *chtype* variable.

PLOP DOWN AN ALTERNATIVE CHARACTER

The following code uses the A_ALTCHARSET attribute to display the value of *pi*.

04-04_pi.c

```
1    #include <ncurses.h>
2
3    int main()
4    {
5    initscr();
6
7        addch(A_ALTCHARSET | ACS_PI);
8        addstr(" = 3.14159");
9        refresh();
10       getch();
11
12       endwin();
13       return(0);
14   }
```

The *addch()* function in Line 7 merges the A_ALTCHARSET attribute with the alternative character set constant for the *pi* character. Here's the output:

```
π = 3.14159
```

Not every terminal outputs the *pi* character. If not, an asterisk appears instead.

ALTERNATIVE CHARACTER LIST

A list of common alternative characters is defined in the ncurses.h file. Table 4-3 lists the characters' defined names, the alternative character, it's ASCII fallback, and a description.

DEFINE NAME	CHAR	CODE HEX/ CHAR	ALT	DESCRIPTION
ACS_BLOCK	■	0x30 '0'	#	A solid (100%) block
ACS_BOARD	▓	0x65 'h'	#	Border of squares
ACS_BTEE	⊥	0x76 'v'	+	Line art bottom T intersection
ACS_BULLET	•	0x7E '~'	o	Bullet
ACS_CKBOARD	▒	0x61 'a'	:	Checkerboard
ACS_DARROW	↓	0x2E '.'	v	Down arrow
ACS_DEGREE	°	0x66 'f'	'	Degree symbol
ACS_DIAMOND	◊	0x60 '`'	+	Diamond
ACS_GEQUAL	≥	0x7A 'z'	>	Greater-than-or-equal-to
ACS_HLINE	—	0x71 'q'	-	Line art horizontal line
ACS_LANTERN	§	0x 69 'i'	#	Lantern or section symbol
ACS_LARROW	←	0x2C ','	<	Left arrow
ACS_LEQUAL	≤	0x79 'y'	<	Less-than-or-equal-to
ACS_LLCORNER	└	0x6D 'm'	+	Line art lower left corner
ACS_LRCORNER	┘	0x6A 'j'	+	Line art lower right corner
ACS_LTEE	├	0x74 't'	+	Line art left T intersection
ACS_NEQUAL	≠	0x7C '|'	!	Not equal
ACS_PI	π	0x7B '{'	*	Pi
ACS_PLMINUS	±	0x67 'g'	#	Plus/minus

ACS_PLUS	+	0x6E 'n'	+	Large plus or crossover
ACS_RARROW	→	0x2B '+'	>	Right arrow
ACS_RTEE	⊣	0x75 'u'	+	Line art right T intersection
ACS_S1 ... ACS_S9		0x6F 'o' ... 0x73 's'	-	Scan lines 1 (top) through 9 (bottom)
ACS_STERLING	£	0x7D '}'	f	British pound
ACS_TTEE	⊤	0x77 'w'	+	Line art top T intersection
ACS_UARROW	↑	0x2D '-'	^	Up arrow
ACS_ULCORNER	⌐	0x6C 'l'	+	Line art upper left corner
ACS_URCORNER	⌐	0x6B 'k'	+	Line art upper right corner
ACS_VLINE	|	0x78 'x'	|	Line art vertical line

Table 4-3. The Alternative Character Set.

The characters shown in Table 4-3 are approximations of what you see on the terminal screen and they may not appear correctly in this eBook. (eBooks are formatted best for summer potboilers, not technical information.) Refer to this book's companion website for the full table:

http://www.c-for-dummies.com/ncurses/

When a character isn't available, an alternative is used as shown in the Alt column. Further, you might find the character is available, but not accessible via Ncurses' alternative character set. In that situation, you must use other code to display the special character, such as the Unicode examples shown later in this Chapter.

Wide or *char_t* constants are identical to those listed in the table, though with the prefix W added to the defined name. For example, the wide plus/minus character is defined as WACS_PLMINUS.

YOUR TERMINAL'S ACS REVIEW

The following code lets you view which alternative characters
are available for your terminal.

04-05_acslist.c

```
1    #include <ncurses.h>
2
3    int main()
4    {
5         int a;
6
7         initscr();
8
9         for(a=0;a<127;a++)
10        {
11             printw("\t%2X:",a);
12             addch(A_ALTCHARSET | a);
13        }
14        refresh();
15        getch();
16
17        endwin();
18        return(0);
19   }
```

The *for* loop at Line 9 plows through ASCII codes 0 through 127.
Each code value is displayed at line 11, then an *addch()* function
displays the *chtype* character from the alternative character set.

Output varies, depending on the terminal.

ASC STRING OUTPUT

When you need to display a string of ASC characters, set the
A_ALTCHARSET attribute first, then output the text. This process
is like shooting in the dark, because unless you've memorized
the ASC/ASCII alternatives, the results can be strange.

04_06_acsstring.c

```
1    #include <ncurses.h>
2
3    int main()
4    {
5         initscr();
6
7         attrset(A_ALTCHARSET);
8         addstr("Hello there!");
9         refresh();
10        getch();
11
12        endwin();
13        return(0);
```

```
14        }
```

To activate the alternative character set, the *attrset()* function in Line 7 applies the **A_ALTCHARSET** attribute. The *addstr()* function outputs text with that attribute active.

BUILD A BOX

The following code spews out individual characters to create a box on the screen. Ncurses has a *box()* function that does the same thing, which I introduce in a <u>later chapter</u>, but you can manually create a box by using the individual ACS characters as shown in this example.

04-07_abox.c

```
1     #include <ncurses.h>
2
3     int main()
4     {
5             initscr();
6
7             addch(ACS_ULCORNER);
8             addch(ACS_HLINE);
9             addch(ACS_URCORNER);
10            addch('\n');
11            addch(ACS_VLINE);
12            addch(' ');
13            addch(ACS_VLINE);
14            addch('\n');
15            addch(ACS_LLCORNER);
16            addch(ACS_HLINE);
17            addch(ACS_LRCORNER);
18            addch('\n');
19            refresh();
20            getch();
21
22            endwin();
23            return(0);
24    }
```

This code clumsily puts a set of alternative characters to the screen. It contains 12 lines of *addch()* functions, one after the other. The output resembles a box.

Because the ACS character definitions are used directly, you don't need to set the **A_ALTCHARSET** attribute. The ACS definitions include that attribute, along with the character codes required to generate the box-drawing symbols.

The *chtype* Array

The *chtype* is a variable, but if you try to build a string of *chtype* characters, you might find that Ncurses doesn't output that text. That's because a *chtype* isn't a *char* and an array of *chtype* variables isn't a string.

DISPLAY THE ARRAY ONE CHARACTER AT A TIME

To display a "string" of *chtype* variables, you first concoct the "string." For example:

```
chtype string[] = {
        'H' | A_BOLD, 'e', 'l' | A_REVERSE,
        'l' | A_REVERSE, 'o', '!' | A_UNDERLINE,
        0
};
```

Each element in the *chtype* array is a *chtype* character, which can be either a *char* variable directly, a value, or a logical operation to present attributes and characters.

04-08_chtypestring.c

```
1    #include <ncurses.h>
2
3    int main()
4    {
5            chtype string[] = {
6                    'H' | A_BOLD, 'e', 'l' | A_REVERSE,
7                    'l' | A_REVERSE, 'o', '!' | A_UNDERLINE,
8                    0
9            };
10           int x = 0;
11
12           initscr();
13
14           while(string[x])
15           {
16                   addch(string[x]);
17                   x++;
18           }
19           refresh();
20           getch();
21
22           endwin();
23           return(0);
24   }
```

In this code, the *chtype* array `string[]` is displayed one character at a time, thanks to the *addch()* function at Line 16. The *while* loop uses the zero value at the end of the array to terminate the loop.

Attributes in a *chtype* character apply only to that character. Therefore, each element in the array must have attributes set as they don't carry over to the next character.

DISPLAY A CHTYPE "STRING"

The array defined in 04-08_chtypestring.c isn't really a string, but Ncurses can see it that way. The *addchstr()* function recognizes *chtype* arrays as strings and displays them as such. The sole argument is a *chtype* array, which must end in value zero or the null character '\0'.

04-09_addchstr.c

```
1    #include <ncurses.h>
2
3    int main()
4    {
5        chtype string[] = {
6            'H' | A_BOLD, 'e', 'l' | A_REVERSE,
7            'l' | A_REVERSE, 'o', '!' | A_UNDERLINE,
8            0
9        };
10
11       initscr();
12
13       addchstr(string);
14       refresh();
15       getch();
16
17       endwin();
18       return(0);
19   }
```

This example generates the same output as the previous one, but with fewer lines. That's because the *addchstr()* function at Line 13 processes the string[] array automatically.

AN ACS *CHTYPE* ARRAY

A *chtype* array can also contain ACS characters, as the ACS is also a *chtype*. If you review the code in 04-07_abox.c, you see multiple statements that cry out for a *chtype* array:

```
chtype box[12] = {
    ACS_ULCORNER, ACS_HLINE, ACS_URCORNER, '\n',
    ACS_VLINE, ' ', ACS_VLINE, '\n',
    ACS_LLCORNER, ACS_HLINE, ACS_LRCORNER, 'n'
};
```

The box[] array is defined as a *chtype*. Good. It lists ACS constants plus some standard text. Good. And it's the right size and so on. All good.

Yet, if you loop through the array as was done in 04–08_chtypestring.c, you won't get the same output as for 04–07_abox.c. That's because the ACS constants are expanded during compile time and the results aren't useful in your code.

The solution in this case is to use the values or characters to which the ACS characters are assigned. The Code column in Table 4-3 lists the values and characters you can use, but you must apply the A_ALTCHARSET attribute to each one to make it work.

In the following example, I use the *attrset()* function to apply the A_ALTCHARSET attribute to the standard screen window. Then the characters in the box[] array output as ACS, not plain text.

04-10_boxarray.c

```
1    #include <ncurses.h>
2
3    int main()
4    {
5         char box[] = "lqk\nx x\nmqj\n";
6
7         initscr();
8
9         attrset(A_ALTCHARSET);
10        addstr(box);
11        refresh();
12        getch();
13
14        endwin();
15        return(0);
16   }
```

The box string in Line 5 looks odd, but those characters are equivalent to the ACS characters used to draw a box. After the proper attribute is set in Line 9, the *addstr()* function outputs the box.

Fortunately, the need to output alternative characters isn't always string-related. Mostly, they're one-off characters, which you can easily put to the display by using an *addch()* function.

45

Unicode Output

Ncurses can output Unicode text the same as any C program sends Unicode to standard output. It's not a straightforward operation, but it can be done.

NCURSES AND UNICODE

First, you must ensure that the constant `_XOPEN_SOURCE_EXTENDED` is defined as 1. This definition must take place before the `ncurses.h` header file is included in the source code.

Second, you must set the locale to incorporate the Unicode character set in the program's output. Use the *setlocale()* function, defined in `locale.h`, similar to the following:

```
setlocale(LC_CTYPE,"en_US.UTF-8");
```

Above, I'm using `en_US` for English-United States.

Finally, you use the Ncurses wide-character output function *add_wch()*. It's the equivalent of the *addch()* function:

```
add_wch(*wch)
```

The `wch` argument is the address of a *cchar_t* structure. It's not a "Unicode character," but a two-member structure that contains an attribute and a wide character array:

```
typedef struct {
      attr_t attr;
      wchar_t        chars[CCHARW_MAX];
} cchar_t;
```

The `attr` member is an attribute, such as `A_NORMAL`.

The `chars` member is a *wchar_t* (wide character) array of the length set by the `CCHARW_MAX` constant, which is defined as 5 on my system. This member contains the Unicode code of the character to display, specified as a spacing character followed by non-spacing characters with a long null character terminating, `L'\0'`.

The *add_wch()* function features variations with the *w*, *mv*, and *mvw* prefixes for output to a named window, at a given line/column position, or a mixture of both, respectively.

04-11_unicode.c

```
1   #define _XOPEN_SOURCE_EXTENDED 1
2   #include <ncurses.h>
3   #include <locale.h>
4
5   int main()
6   {
7       cchar_t heart = {
8           A_NORMAL,
9           L"\u2665"
10      };
11
12      /* activate Unicode character set */
13      setlocale(LC_CTYPE,"en_US.UTF-8");
14
15      initscr();
16
17      addstr("I ");
18      add_wch(&heart);
19      addstr(" Ncurses");
20      refresh();
21      getch();
22
23      endwin();
24      return(0);
25  }
```

The _XOPEN_SOURCE_EXTENDED constant is set to 1 at Line 1, before the ncurses.h header is included in the source code. If you fail to do this, the compiler may complain about the *add_wch()* function.

Line 7 creates the *cchar_t* structure heart, and assigns to it values A_NORMAL (as the attribute) and Unicode character code 0x2665 as the character.

The *setlocale()* function at Line 13 preps output for Unicode text.

Lines 17 through 19 display a message, with Line 18 using the *add_wch()* function to display the Unicode character defined in the heart structure. The & (ampersand) is used to fetch the structure's address, making it a pointer.

Here is sample output:

```
I ♥ Ncurses
```

UNICODE STRINGS

You don't need to concoct an array of *cchar_t* structures to output a string of Unicode text. Instead, use the *addwstr()* function. It requires an array of *wchar_t* (wide character) elements. This function makes the Unicode output process simpler than using *add_wch()* and the *cchar_t* structure.

04-12_ustring.c

```
1    #define _XOPEN_SOURCE_EXTENDED 1
2    #include <ncurses.h>
3    #include <locale.h>
4
5    int main()
6    {
7        wchar_t hello[] = {
8            0x041f, 0x0440, 0x0438,
9            0x0432, 0x0435, 0x0442,
10           0x0021, 0x0
11       };
12
13       setlocale(LC_CTYPE,"en_US.UTF-8");
14
15       initscr();
16
17       addwstr(hello);
18       refresh();
19       getch();
20
21       endwin();
22       return(0);
23   }
```

A *wchar_t* array `hello[]` is declared at Line 7. It consists of Unicode values, ending with a zero. The *addwstr()* function at Line 17 displays the `hello[]` array.

Here is the output:

Привет!

(That's Russian for "Hello" or "Greetings.")

♦ *If you don't see the text output in Cygwin, change the font to* Lucida Console *or some other font that supports Unicode text.*

To apply attributes to the Unicode text, use the *attrset()* or *attron()* function before issuing the *addwstr()* function. And as with most Ncurses output functions, a *w, mv,* and *wmv* variations of the *addwstr()* function are available.

5. Cursor Here or There

Full-screen control really means setting the cursor's location. Rather than march left-to-right and down the screen, Ncurses lets you change the cursor's position to any valid location on the screen. Once set, you can then place individual characters or strings.

The Screen's Size

The traditional PC terminal window displayed characters in 25 rows of 80 columns. That's typical, but it may not be the dimensions of an xterm window in Linux or the command prompt in Windows. Before you can plot the cursor's position, it helps to know the screen size and, therefore, the limits of where the cursor can go.

THE WINDOW IS Y BY X CHARACTERS

To discover the size of any window in Ncurses, use the *getmax()* function:

```
getmaxyx(stdscr,y,x)
```

Above, the size of the window `stdscr` is returned in variables `y` and `x`, where `y` is the row count and `x` is the column count. The name of the function, *getmaxyx()*, helps you remember that Y, or rows, comes first.

The standard screen, `stdscr`, is the default output screen in Ncurses. It's the same size as the terminal window.

Integer variables `y` and `x` are *not* pointers. They hold the dimensions of the named window after the function call. Also, the values indicate the number of rows and columns, so they start at 1, not zero.

05-01_screensize.c

```
1   #include <ncurses.h>
2
3   int main()
4   {
5       int x,y;
6
7       initscr();
```

```
8
9               getmaxyx(stdscr,y,x);
10              printw("Window is %d rows by %d columns.\n",
11                  y,x);
12              refresh();
13              getch();
14
15              endwin();
16              return(0);
17        }
```

Here's what I see for output:

```
Windows is 24 rows, 80 columns.
```

Because my computer's terminal window roosts in a graphical operating system, I can re-size it. After I do, running the program again yields the new window size:

```
Windows is 64 rows, 132 columns.
```

♦ *Use the* getmaxyx() *function at the start of your code to determine the window's size. Never guess the size.*

AND NOW: THE SHORTCUT

The *getmaxyx()* function reads the dimensions of any Ncurses window. Because the standard screen is special, its size is kept in two constants: LINES and COLS.

The value of LINES equals the number of rows (Y) on the standard screen.

The value of COLS equals the number of columns (X) on the standard screen.

05-02_stdscrsize.c

```
1     #include <ncurses.h>
2
3     int main()
4     {
5             initscr();
6
7             printw("Window is %d rows by %d columns.\n",
8                 LINES,COLS);
9             refresh();
10            getch();
11
12            endwin();
13            return(0);
14      }
```

The output is the same as from the code for 05-01_screensize.c, though LINES and COLS are always specific to the standard screen.

♦ *Remember that the Y constant is LINES and not ROWS.*

Move the Cursor

The cursor's location on the screen is affected by any function that outputs text. Further, some characters can change the cursor's position, such as the newline (\n) and the backspace (\b). To deliberately set the cursor's location, use the *move()* function:

```
move(y,x)
```

Variable y represents a row or line position; variable x is a column. Location 0, 0 is the upper left corner of the screen or window.

A typical *move()* function is followed by a text-output function. To save time, most text-output functions combine moving the cursor, such as:

```
mvaddch(y,x,ch)
```

```
mvaddstr(y,x,*str)
```

```
mvprintw(y,x,format,arg[…])
```

The function's *mv* prefix means that the first two arguments are a row (y) and column (x). The rest of the function's arguments are the same as for the original function.

CORNERED!

Each window on the text screen features four corners: upper left, upper right, lower left and lower right. Using data from the *getmaxyx()* function, along with the *mvaddch()* function, you can plot characters in each of the corners.

05-03_corners.c

```
1    #include <ncurses.h>
2
3    int main()
4    {
5    int lines,cols;
6
7        initscr();
```

```
 8          getmaxyx(stdscr,lines,cols);
 9          lines--;
10          cols--;
11
12          mvaddch(0,0,'*');                /* UL corner */
13          refresh();
14          napms(500);                      /* pause 1/2 sec */
15
16          mvaddch(0,cols,'*');             /* UR corner */
17          refresh();
18          napms(500);
19
20          mvaddch(lines,0,'*');            /* LL corner */
21          refresh();
22          napms(500);
23
24          mvaddch(lines,cols,'*');             /* LR corner */
25          refresh();
26          getch();
27
28          endwin();
29          return(0);
30      }
```

The program uses the *mvaddch()* function to slap down an asterisk in every corner of the standard screen.

Line 12 could have been re-written as just:

```
mvaddch('*');                /* UL corner */
```

That's because Ncurses initializes the cursor at the *home* location of 0,0 for each of its windows.

CENTER THAT TITLE!

When you know a window's width, you can write code to center a line of text. The process works like this:

1. Retrieve the screen width and text width.

2. Subtract the text width from the screen width and divide the result by two.

4. Use the *move()* function to set the cursor and offset the text at the position calculated in Step 2.

Here's sample code:

05-04_ctitle.c

```
1      #include <ncurses.h>
2      #include <string.h>
3
4      void center(int row, char *title);
5
```

```
 6      int main()
 7      {
 8              initscr();
 9
10              center(1, "Penguin Soccer Finals");
11              center(5, "Cattle Dung Samples from Temecula");
12              center(7, "Catatonic Theater");
13              center(9, "Why Do Ions Hate Each Other?");
14              getch();
15
16              endwin();
17              return(0);
18      }
19
20      void center(int row, char *title)
21      {
22              int len,indent,y,width;
23
24              /* get screen width */
25              getmaxyx(stdscr,y,width);
26              /* get title length */
27              len = strlen(title);
28              /* calculate indent */
29              indent = (width - len)/2;
30              /* show the string */
31              mvaddstr(row,indent,title);
32              refresh();
33      }
```

The *center()* function's arguments are the line (row) number and the text to be centered on that line.

♦ *The window's top row is zero, not 1.*

Starting at Line 20, the *center()* function obtains the screen size, then obtains the string's length. In Line 29, the math calculates the indent.

A *mvaddstr()* function at Line 31 displays the string at the proper position.

No error-checking is done in this code to ensure that the string isn't wider than the window. If I were to release the *center()* function into the wild, I'd definitely confirm that the `indent` variable isn't less than zero.

Where is the Cursor?

Just as you can move the cursor, Ncurses also lets you discover the cursor's current location. The function is *getyx()*:

```
getyx(win,y,x)
```

The first argument is the window, such as `stdscr` for the standard screen. The next two arguments are *int* variables – not pointers – which store the cursor's line and column position after the function call.

As with other cursor functions, such as *move()*, remember that the home location is 0,0, the upper left corner of the window.

05-05_whereami.c

```
1    #include <ncurses.h>
2
3    int main()
4    {
5            char ch='\0';                 /* initialize ch */
6            int row,col;
7
8            initscr();
9
10           addstr("Type some text; '~' to end:\n");
11           refresh();
12
13           while( (ch=getch()) != '~')
14                   ;
15
16           getyx(stdscr,row,col);
17           printw("\n\nThe cursor was at position %d, %d "
18                   ,row,col);
19           printw("when you stopped typing.");
20           refresh();
21           getch();
22
23           endwin();
24           return(0);
25   }
```

As the program runs, type away. Tap the ~ (tilde) key to stop typing and fetch the cursor's location, which is reported in the output. For example:

```
Type some text; '~' to end:
Bill is a jerk!~

The cursor was at row 1, column 15
When you stopped typing.
```

The position reported is relative to the home location, 0, 0. So if you (a human) were to count the cursor's position, you'd come up with row 2, column 16 for the result.

Also note that the cursor's position is fetched after the ~ character is displayed.

♦ *The function is named* getyx()*, not* getxy()*. The Y or line value comes first, which is typical for most Ncurses functions that deal with screen coordinates.*

6. Text Manipulation

With full-control over the terminal screen and cursor's location, you might plan on doing some full-screen text manipulation, such as inserting a line of text, deleting a chunk of text, and other fancy feats. Don't bother. That's because Ncurses comes with handy text manipulation functions built-in.

Insert Text Functions

The functions that add text to the screen, such as *addch()*, *addstr()*, and *printw()*, place text at the cursor's position. Any existing text is overwritten. To preserve the text, you must first insert some space. The two functions that make this happen are *insertln()* and *insch()*.

```
insertln()
```

```
insch(ch)
```

The *insertln()* function inserts a blank line of text at a given line on the screen at the cursor's current row. All text below the new line scrolls down, with the bottom line removed (not saved). The cursor's position is unchanged by the *insertln()* function.

The *insch()* function inserts a single character at the cursor's location, specified as *chtype* argument ch. The new character appears at the cursor's location and the cursor advances. Any text to the right of the cursor is moved forward one space. Text doesn't wrap; the character shoved off the far-right column is forgotten.

CHAPTER CODE SAMPLE

The following code serves as the core for the rest of this chapter's samples.

06-01_text1.c

```
1    #include <ncurses.h>
2
3    int main()
4    {
5        char text1[] = "This is the first line\n";
6        char text2[] = "Line two here\n";
7        char text3[] = "The third line\n";
```

```
8              char text4[] = "Fourth line here\n";
9              char text5[] = "And the fifth line\n";
10
11     initscr();
12
13     addstr(text1);
14     addstr(text3);
15     addstr(text5);
16     refresh();
17     getch();
18
19     endwin();
20     return(0);
21     }
```

Only the odd-numbered strings are output:

```
This is the first line
The third line
And the fifth line
```

♦ *If you compile with the* -Wall *or* -Wunused-variable *switch, a warning appears about unused variables. This warning is expected.*

NEW BLANK LINES

In the following code, the *insertln()* function adds a blank line at row 1. (Zero is the top row.) The *inesrtln()* function doesn't add text; it merely makes room at the cursor's current location (row), as the following code demonstrates:

06-02_text2.c

```
1      #include <ncurses.h>
2
3      int main()
4      {
5              char text1[] = "This is the first line\n";
6              char text2[] = "Line two here\n";
7              char text3[] = "The third line\n";
8              char text4[] = "Fourth line here\n";
9              char text5[] = "And the fifth line\n";
10
11             initscr();
12
13             addstr(text1);
14             addstr(text3);
15             addstr(text5);
16             refresh();
17             getch();
18
19             move(1,0);        /* Second line/row */
20             insertln();       /* add a blank line */
21             refresh();
22             getch();
23
```

```
24              endwin();
25              return(0);
26          }
```

The code added to the chapter's first code example (06–01_text1.c) is highlighted above.

Line 19 moves the cursor to the first position on the second line, location 1, 0. The *insertln()* function at Line 20 adds the blank line, moving any text down a row on the screen. Then the screen is refreshed so you can see the results, which look like this:

```
This is the first line

The third line
And the fifth line
```

The cursor blinks at the start of the second line.

Because the *insertln()* function doesn't add text, if you want to insert the string text2[] into the new, blank line, you must further modify the code:

06-03_text3.c

```
1     #include <ncurses.h>
2
3     int main()
4     {
5         char text1[] = "This is the first line\n";
6         char text2[] = "Line two here\n";
7         char text3[] = "The third line\n";
8         char text4[] = "Fourth line here\n";
9         char text5[] = "And the fifth line\n";
10
11        initscr();
12
13        addstr(text1);
14        addstr(text3);
15        addstr(text5);
16        refresh();
17        getch();
18
19        move(1,0);       /* Second line/row */
20        insertln();      /* add a blank line */
21        refresh();
22        getch();
23
24        addstr(text2);
25        refresh();
26        getch();
27
28        endwin();
29        return(0);
30    }
```

At Line 24, the `text2[]` string is added at the cursor's location, which is the start of the second row.

EXERCISE 06-04_TEXT4.C

Complete the code by inserting two blank lines at the second step. So, the user presses a key and blank rows 1 and 3 open. Then strings `text2[]` and `text4[]` are inserted.

INSERT ONE CHARACTER AT A TIME

The *insch()* function works like *insertln()*, but horizontally instead of vertically and by a single character only. The character can be a single *char* value, or a full *chtype* variable.

In the following code, *insch()* inserts characters on a line in a manner that emulates a scrolling marquee.

06-05_marquee1.c

```
1    #include <ncurses.h>
2    #include <string.h>
3
4    int main()
5    {
6         char text[] = "Armstrong walks on moon!";
7         char *t;
8         int len;
9
10        initscr();
11
12        len = strlen(text);
13        t = text;                    /* initialize pointer */
14        while(len)
15        {
16             move(5,5);              /* insert same spot */
17             insch(*(t+len-1));      /* work backwards */
18             refresh();
19             napms(100);             /* .1 sec. delay */
20             len--;
21        }
22        getch();
23
24        endwin();
25        return(0);
26    }
```

String `text[]` is displayed one character at a time in the *while* loop starting at Line 14. Each character is inserted at position 5,5 (Line 16) with the *insch()* function at Line 17. The pointer math in the function reads the string from the last character to the first. The effect is a scrolling marquee.

The following modifies the preceding source code, filling the existing row with text so that you can more graphically see how the *insch()* function inserts characters.

06-06_marquee2.c

```
1    #include <ncurses.h>
2    #include <string.h>
3
4    int main()
5    {
6         char text[] = "Armstrong walks on moon!";
7         char *t;
8         char a;
9         int len;
10
11        initscr();
12
13        /* display a line of text */
14        move(5,0);
15        for(a='A';a<'Z'+1;a++)
16        {
17             addch(a);
18             addstr("  ");  /* two spaces */
19        }
20
21        len = strlen(text);
22        t = text;       /* initialize pointer */
23        while(len)
24        {
25             move(5,5);      /* insert same spot */
26             insch(*(t+len-1));      /* work backwards */
27             refresh();
28             napms(100);     /* .1 sec. delay */
29             len--;
30        }
31        getch();
32
33        endwin();
34        return(0);
35   }
```

Line 14 locates the cursor to the start of row 6. A *for* loop splashes down letters 'A' through 'Z' two spaces apart, which fills the line with something visible. When the marquee is displayed (Lines 23 through 30), you can see how the inserted text pushes existing text to the right.

INSERTING A STRING OF TEXT

The *insstr()* function works like *insch()*, but with an entire string and not just a single character:

```
insstr(*str)
```

Argument `str` is a standard, null-character terminated string or *char* array. It's inserted one character at a time on the screen, shoving any existing text to the right. (The *insstr()* function is a macro that repeatedly the *insch()* function to display a string of text.)

06-07_TEXT5.C

```
1    #include <ncurses.h>
2
3    int main()
4    {
5            char text1[] = "This is the first line\n";
6            char text2[] = "Line two here\n";
7            char text3[] = "The third line\n";
8            char text4[] = "Fourth line here\n";
9            char text5[] = "And the fifth line\n";
10
11           initscr();
12
13           addstr(text1);
14           addstr(text3);
15           addstr(text5);
16           refresh();
17           getch();
18
19           move(1,0);
20           insstr(text2);
21           refresh();
22           getch();
23
24           endwin();
25           return(0);
26   }
```

The *insstr()* function at Line 20 inserts string `text2` at the cursor's location, row 1 (line 2), column 0. Here's the output:

```
This is the first line
Line two here
And the fifth line
```

You may have noticed that `text3` was overwritten, not pushed to the right. That's because the `text2` string ends with a newline character. When displayed (or inserted), that character erases text to the end of the line.

To fix the code, remove the newline character from the end of Line 6.

Here's the output from the fixed code:

```
This is the first line
Line two hereThe third line
And the fifth line
```

The text "The third line" is pushed to the right as string `text2` is inserted.

Delete Text Functions

To remove a text from the screen, use the *deleteln()* and *delch()* functions. Of the two, *delch()* is my favorite because I can pronounce it:

```
deletln()
```

```
delch()
```

The *deleteln()* removes the current row, where the cursor is set. Text below the line is scrolled up a line to fill in the gap. A blank line appears at the bottom of the window.

The *delch()* function removes a character at the cursor's position. Text to the right of the cursor shimmies over one character position. A blank is inserted at the end of the row.

REMOVE A LINE OF TEXT

The following code uses *deleteln()* to remove a line of text from the window.

06-08_text6.c

```
1    #include <ncurses.h>
2
3    int main()
4    {
5        initscr();
6
7        /* add five lines */
8        addstr("This is the first line\n");
9        addstr("Line two here\n");
10       addstr("The third line\n");
11       addstr("Fourth line here\n");
12       addstr("And the fifth line\n");
13       refresh();
14       getch();
15
```

```
16              /* remove a line*/
17              move(2,0);
18              deleteln();
19              refresh();
20              getch();
21
22              endwin();
23              return(0);
24      }
```

First, the five lines appear on the screen:

```
This is the first line
Line two here
The third line
Fourth line here
And the fifth line
```

The cursor blinks at the start of the sixth line, row 5. So, in the code, at Line 23, a *move()* function relocates the cursor to the third line. Then the *deleteln()* function removes that line, with the following text scrolling up to fill the blank row. Here's the final display:

```
This is the first line
Line two here
Fourth line here
And the fifth line
```

The *deleteln()* function doesn't affect the cursor's location, so in the program, the cursor remains at the start of the third row (line 2).

REMOVE A CHARACTER

In the following example, five lines of text are put to the standard screen. The *delch()* function is then used to remove the word `line` from the fourth line (third row).

06-09_text7.c

```
1       #include <ncurses.h>
2
3       int main()
4       {
5               int x;
6
7               initscr();
8
9               addstr("This is the first line\n");
10              addstr("Line two here\n");
11              addstr("The third line\n");
12              addstr("Fourth line here\n");
13              addstr("And the fifth line\n");
14              refresh();
```

```
15          getch();
16
17          move(3,7);
18          for(x=0;x<5;x++)
19          {
20                  delch();
21                  refresh();
22                  napms(250);
23          }
24          getch();
25
26          endwin();
27          return(0);
28      }
```

The cursor is positioned at Line 17. The *delch()* function doesn't move the cursor, so you don't need to update its position in the *for* loop (Line 18).

The *delch()* function repeats five times to remove the word `line`, plus the following space. At Line 22, the *napms()* function pauses for a quarter second so that you can see the word erased.

EXERCISE 06-10_CAT.C

Write code to display the following line:

`Where did that silly cat go?`

After the user presses any key, they see the word `silly` erased one character at a time, then it's replaced by the word `fat` one character at a time.

A Dual Insert and Delete Function

The *insdelln()* function inserts or deletes lines of text from the screen, depending on its argument.

`insdelln(n)`

For positive values of n, a given number of lines are inserted. For negative values, lines are removed. The lines inserted or removed are relative to the cursor's location, and the function doesn't alter that location.

The `insdelln(1)` statement is identical to *insertln()*.

The `insdelln(-1)` statement call is identical to *deleteln()*.

Of course, you can specify values other than 1 and -1, as the following code demonstrates.

06-11_insdel.c

```
1      #include <ncurses.h>
2
3      int main()
4      {
5              int row,col;
6
       initscr();
8
9              for(row=0;row<LINES;row++)
10                     for(col=0;col<COLS;col++)
11                             addch('.');
12             refresh();
13             getch();
14
15             move(5,0);
16             insdelln(3);
17             refresh();
18             getch();
19
20             insdelln(-5);
21             refresh();
22             getch();
23
24             endwin();
25             return(0);
26     }
```

Lines 9 through 11 fill the screen with periods. That way you can see the effect as rows are inserted and removed.

At Line 15, the cursor is located at row 6, first column. In Line 16, the *insdelln()* function inserts 3 new lines. The effect is that you see three blank rows appear on the screen; the periods on the lines below are pushed down.

After the user presses a key, the *insdelln()* function at Line 30 removes 5 lines from the screen. The remaining lines are pulled up, revealing blanks at the bottom of the screen.

♦ *When* insdelln() *is called with zero as its argument, nothing happens.*

7. Clear and Zap

When you create a new window in Ncurses, it's blank. Then you fill it with text or something else fun and exciting. When you need some or all of the window blank again, you rely upon one of the clearing and zapping functions, such as *erase()*, *clear()*, *clrtoeol()*, and *clrtobot()*.

Erase the Window

Two functions are available to clear or erase a window or screen in Ncurses: `clear()`

`erase()`

Both the functions end up doing the same thing, so why two?

The *erase()* function is faster but less thorough.

The *clear()* function has more overhead, but it's my favorite.

07-01_cls.c

```
1    #include <ncurses.h>
2
3    int main()
4    {
5            int c,y,x,cmax;
6
7            initscr();
8
9            getmaxyx(stdscr,y,x);
10           cmax = (x * y) / 5;
11           for(c=0;c<cmax;c++)
12                   addstr("blah ");
13           refresh();
14           getch();
15
16           clear();        /* clear the screen */
17           refresh();      /* don't forget this! */
18           getch();
19
20           endwin();
21           return(0);
22   }
```

The code uses the *getmaxyx()* function at Line 9 to grab the screen size. A calculation is made (Line 10) to determine the maximum number of times the text "`blah `" (with a space) can be put to the standard screen. A *for* loop fills the screen in Lines 11 and 12, then the screen is refreshed and the user must press a key.

At Line 16, the *clear()* function clears the screen.

♦ *Don't forget the* refresh() *after you clear! The screen is cleared, but only when you update the standard screen (or other window) does the user see the effect.*

If you substitute the *erase()* function at Line 16, the effect is the same.

Clrto means "Clear to"

When you must clear only part of the screen, use the *clrtoeol()* or *clrtobot()* functions.

```
clrtoeol()
```

```
clrtobot()
```

The *clrtoeol()* function clears from the cursor's position to the end of the current line. Think, "Clear to end of line."

The *clrtobot()* function clears from the cursor's current position to the bottom of the screen. Think, "clear to bottom."

Neither function affects the cursor's position.

CLEAR TO THE END OF THE LINE

To remove an entire line, or just from the cursor's location to the end of a line, use the *clrtoeol()* function. Unlike the *deleteln()* function, *clrtoeol()* erases only part of a line and doesn't affect line below.

07-02_clearline.c

```
1    #include <ncurses.h>
2
3    int main()
4    {
5        int c,y,x,cmax;
6
7        initscr();
8
9        getmaxyx(stdscr,y,x);
10       cmax = (x * y) / 5;
11       for(c=0;c<cmax;c++)
12           addstr("blah ");
13       refresh();
14       getch();
```

```
15
16              move(5,20);     /* Setup the cursor */
17              clrtoeol();     /* Clear to end of line */
18              refresh();
19              getch();
20
21              endwin();
22              return(0);
23       }
```

As with the earlier example, `07-01_cls.c`, Lines 9 through 12 fill the standard screen with "`blah` " text. The program waits for the user to press at key at Line 14.

At Line 16, the cursor is moved to location 5, 20 – the sixth line, 21st column over. The *clrtoeol()* function at Line 17 clears from that location to the end of the line.

CLEAR TO THE BOTTOM OF THE WINDOW

The *clrtobot()* function replaces all the text from the cursor's position to the last position on the screen with blanks (spaces).

♦   *BOT means Bottom Of Text.*

The following code is a one-line modification to `07-02_clearline.c`. In this version, Line 17 is replaced with the *clrtobot()* function.

07-03_clearbot.c

```
1        #include <ncurses.h>
2
3        int main()
4        {
5              int c,y,x,cmax;
6
7              initscr();
8
9              getmaxyx(stdscr,y,x);
10             cmax = (x * y) / 5;
11             for(c=0;c<cmax;c++)
12                  addstr("blah ");
13             refresh();
14             getch();
15
16             move(5,20);     /* Setup the cursor */
17             clrtobot()      /* Clear to bottom */
18             refresh();
19             getch();
20
21             endwin();
22             return(0);
23       }
```

Unlike the *clrtoeol()* example, this code clears from location 5, 20 to the end of the screen – or the bottom of the window.

CLEAR TO THE TOP OF THE SCREEN

Ncurses lacks a function to clear from the cursor's location to the top of the window. Likewise, no function is available to erase text from the cursor's position to the *start* of a line. Like any good programmer, however, you can code such functions on your own.

8. Keyboard Input

Input for a standard C library program may not come from the keyboard. Therefore, the code treats input as a stream. That means it's not interactive; the input stream doesn't pause, and if a buffer overflows, the stream spills into the next buffer (or off into memory).

Input in Ncurses is read directly from the keyboard. Your code can wait for a key to be pressed, scan the buffer for input, or check to see whether any input is pending.

♦ *A text-input function not covered in this chapter is* scanw(), *which works like its standard C library equivalent,* scanf().

Single Character Input

The *getch()* function reads a single character from the keyboard, which is returned as an integer value.

```
int getch()
```

The function either waits for a key to be pressed or it fetches a key waiting in the queue. Unlike the *getchar()* macro in C, you need not press the Enter key for *getch()* to work; any character typed is read immediately.

The value returned by *getch()* is an integer, so variables used should be of the *int* type. I've used *char* variables and not had problems, but *int* is preferred.

The *getch()* function's behavior is affected by other Ncurses functions, such as _echo()_, _keypad()_ and _nodelay()_. These functions are covered elsewhere in this chapter.

READ A SINGLE CHARACTER

The following code uses *getch()* to confirm input with a standard Y-or-N prompt. The code also uses the *getnstr()* function to read a line of input; this function is described <u>later in this chapter</u>.

08-01_yourname.c

```
1   #include <ncurses.h>
2
3   int main()
```

71

```
4       {
5               char name[32];
6               int ch;
7
8               initscr();
9
10              do
11              {
12                      clear();
13                      addstr("Enter your name: ");
14                      getnstr(name,32);
15                      move(1,0);
16                      printw("Your name is %s. ",name);
17                      printw("Is this correct? ");
18                      ch = getch();
19              } while( ch != 'y');
20              move(2,0);
21              printw("Pleased to meet you, %s\n",name);
22              getch();
23
24              endwin();
25              return(0);
26      }
```

The *do-while* loop (Lines 10 through 19) repeats until the **y** key is pressed. Line 13 prompts for the user name. The *getnstr()* function (Line 14) caps input to 31 characters, which truncates a long string preventing overflow of the name buffer.

The *getch()* function at Line 18 immediately reads input – just about any key pressed. If the key isn't a lowercase Y, the loop repeats. Otherwise, Line 21 displays a greeting and execution pauses at Line 22.

Here's sample output:

```
Enter your name: Dan
Your name is Dan. Is this correct? y
Pleased to meet you, Dan
```

If you're astute, you notice that the code is missing a few *refresh()* statements. That's forgivable because the *getch()* function naturally refreshes the screen to display input. Ditto for the *getnstr()* function.

CHECK FOR A KEY PRESS

By default, the *getch()* function pauses for input. This behavior is known as *blocking call*; program execution stops until a key is pressed.

It's possible to change the function's behavior so execution doesn't pause. To do so, you use the *nodelay()* function in the following format:

```
nodelay(win,bf)
```

The `win` argument can be `stdscr` for the standard screen or the name of any valid window. The `bf` argument can be `TRUE` to activate the *getch()* function's non-blocking option, or `FALSE` to restore the default:

```
nodelay(stdscr,TRUE);
```

After the above statement, a *getch()* statement doesn't pause the program's execution. Instead, *getch()* returns either a key waiting in the queue or the `ERR` value, and the program plows ahead.

To restore *getch()* to blocking mode for the standard screen, use this statement:

```
nodelay(stdscr,FALSE);
```

The constants `TRUE`, `FALSE`, and `ERR` are defined in the `ncurses.h` header file.

08-02_keywait1.c

```
1    #include <ncurses.h>
2
3    int main()
4    {
5        int value = 0;
6
7        initscr();
8
9        addstr("Press any key to begin:\n");
10       refresh();
11       getch();
12
13   /* turn off getch() wait */
14       nodelay(stdscr,TRUE);
15       addstr("Press any key to stop the loop!\n");
16       while(getch() == ERR)
17       {
18           printw("%d\r",value++);
19           refresh();
20       }
21
22       endwin();
23       return(0);
24   }
```

The *getch()* function at Line 11 uses its normal, blocking behavior. The program waits for a key to be pressed on the keyboard. (The key's value is unimportant, so it's not saved.)

The *nodelay()* function in Line 14 deactivates *getch()*'s blocking feature. Therefore, the *while* loop repeats until *getch()*returns a value other than ERR, meaning a key is pressed.

EXERCISE 08-03_KEYWAIT2.C

Modify the code from Example 08-02_keywait1.c so that the *while* loop stops only when the spacebar is pressed.

INPUT IN THE DARK

An effect of the *getch()* function is that it echoes the character input to the screen. The *echo()* and *noecho()* functions control this behavior.

```
echo()
noecho()
```

The *echo()* function enables text output as *getch()* reads it, which is the default.

The *noecho()* function suppresses text output as *getch()* reads the keyboard.

These functions affect only whether text input is displayed. They do not alter the *getch()* function's blocking/non-blocking status, plus *getch()* still refreshes the screen when it's issued.

08-04_secretkey.c

```
1    #include <ncurses.h>
2
3    int main()
4    {
5        int key1,key2;
6
7        initscr();
8
9        addstr("Type a key: ");
10       refresh();
11       key1 = getch();
12       clear();
13       addstr("Type the same key: ");
14       noecho();
15       key2 = getch();
16       move(1,0);
```

```
17          if( key1 == key2 )
18                  addstr("The keys match");
19          else
20                  addstr("The keys don't match");
22          getch();
21          refresh();
23
24          endwin();
25          return(0);
26      }
```

The program prompts to type a key, which is read instantly and displayed – but not before the screen clears (Line 12), and you're prompted again to type the same key.

The *noecho()* function at Line 14 disables display of text typed and read by the *getch()* function at Line 15. The *noecho()* condition holds through the rest of the code, so that input at Line 22 isn't displayed either. If an *echo()* function were called before then, then *getch()* would once again display input.

UN-READ A CHARACTER

The *ungetch()* function returns a key (character) to the keyboard queue. This effect is similar to the *ungetc()* function in the standard C library, which returns a character to the input stream.

Why would anyone want to do such a thing?

One reason would be to check the queue. When the *nodelay()* function is active (TRUE), the *getch()* function immediately returns a key from the queue or the constant ERR. If you just want to check the queue, you must use *ungetch()* to return the available key for use later.

This effect of *ungetch()* coupled with *nodelay()* is similar to an old C language function specific to MS-DOS, *kbhit()*. The *kbhit()* function determined whether characters were waiting in the keyboard buffer. If so, the function returned TRUE, otherwise FALSE. You can simulate this behavior in Ncurses.

08-05_kbhit.c

```
1       #include <ncurses.h>
2
3       /* check the keyboard queue */
4       int kbhit()
5       {
6           int ch,r;
7
```

```
 8          /* turn off blocking and echo */
 9                  nodelay(stdscr,TRUE);
10                  noecho();
11
12          /* check for input */
13                  ch = getch();
14                  if( ch == ERR)      /* no input */
15                      r = FALSE;
16                  else                /* input */
17                  {
18                          r = TRUE;
19                          /* return key to queue */
20                          ungetch(ch);
21                  }
22
23          /* restore block and echo */
24                  echo();
25                  nodelay(stdscr,FALSE);
26                  return(r);
27          }
28
29      int main()
30      {
31              int x;
32
33              initscr();
34
35              addstr("Tap a key while I count...\n");
36              for(x=1;x<21;x++)
37              {
38                      printw("%2d ",x);
39                      refresh();
40                      napms(500);
41                      if(kbhit())
42                              break;
43              }
44              addstr("\nDone!\n");
45              printw("You pressed the '%c' key\n",getch());
46              refresh();
47              getch();
48
59              endwin();
50              return(0);
51      }
```

The *kbhit()* function at Line 4 checks the input queue without
reading a character. It does this by modifying the *getch()*
function's behavior: Blocking is removed at Line 9, and echo is
suppressed at Line 10.

Line 13 checks the keyboard queue for input. If ERR is returned,
then the value FALSE is assigned to variable r. Otherwise, at
Line 18, value TRUE is assigned and the character fetched is put
back to the queue in Line 20.

At Line 24, the *getch()* function's default behavior is restored, and the value in r – TRUE or FALSE – is returned.

Within the *main()* function, a *for* loop counts off and displays values. If the *kbhit()* function returns TRUE in Line 41, the loop breaks. The character hasn't been read at this point, it's merely in the queue. Line 45 eventually fetches the character.

ACCESS SPECIAL KEYS

All keys on the computer keyboard generate a code when pressed. The code is returned by key-reading functions, either as the raw code itself or as some other special value as "cooked" by the operating system.

In the case of the alphanumeric keys, the character's ASCII value is returned. For other keys, a 16-bit value, a pair of 8-bit values, or perhaps an escape sequence is returned. Knowing which type of value returned means you can determine exactly which key was pressed, even non-alphanumeric keys. The drawback, of course, is that not every terminal generates the same values.

To retain your sanity, Ncurses offers the *keypad()* function:

```
keypad(win,bf)
```

The win argument can be stdscr for the standard screen or the name of a window. The bf argument is TRUE to activate the feature or FALSE to return to the default.

Once enabled, your program can use defined keyboard constants to read non-alphanumeric keys, as the following code demonstrates.

08-06_arrowkeys.c

```
1    #include <ncurses.h>
2
3    int main()
4    {
5        int ch;
6
7        initscr();
8
9        keypad(stdscr,TRUE);
10       do
11       {
12           ch = getch();
13           switch(ch)
14           {
15               case KEY_DOWN:
```

```
16                              addstr("Down\n");
17                              break;
18                      case KEY_UP:
19                              addstr("Up\n");
20                              break;
21                      case KEY_LEFT:
22                              addstr("Left\n");
23                              break;
24                      case KEY_RIGHT:
25                              addstr("Right\n");
26                      default:
27                              break;
28                      }
29                      refresh();
30              } while(ch != '\n');
31
32              endwin();
33              return(0);
34      }
```

The code modifies *getch()*'s behavior at Line 8. A *do-while* loop spins as any character other than the Enter key is read. If an arrow key is pressed, corresponding text is displayed.

The constants used in the sample code are defined in the ncurses.h header file. Table 7-1 lists the variety.

DEFINITION	KEY
KEY_UP	Cursor up arrow
KEY_DOWN	Cursor down arrow
KEY_LEFT	Cursor left arrow
KEY_RIGHT	Cursor right arrow
KEY_HOME	Home key
KEY_NPAGE	Page Down or Next Page
KEY_PPAGE	Page Up or Previous Page
KEY_END	End key
KEY_BACKSPACE	Backspace key
KEY_F(n)	Function key n

Table 7-1: Special key definitions.

For a function key, replace the n in Table 7-1 with the key number. For example, to check for Function key 5, you would use: KEY_F(5).

Read a String

To read text longer than a single keypress, use the *getstr()* function. Better, use the *getnstr()* function instead, which caps input at *n* characters. Here's the format:

```
getnstr(buf,c)
```

Variable buf is a storage buffer, such as a *char* array, or pointer to a *char* buffer. Value c is the maximum number of characters to type; input halts after c count keystrokes, though you can backspace to edit input. (Unlike stream input, backspace doesn't count as an input character.)

The input count for *getnstr()* should be one less than the size of the storage buffer. So, if the buffer holds 32 characters, use value 31 in the *getnstr()* function.

Press the Enter key to terminate input. The Enter keystroke isn't stored in the buffer.

CONSUME LINES OF TEXT

The following code uses *getnstr()* to read two strings.

08-07_greetings.c

```
1    #include <ncurses.h>
2
3    int main()
4    {
5        char first[32];
6        char last[32];
7
8        initscr();
9
10       addstr("First name: ");
11       getnstr(first,32);
12       addstr("Last name: ");
13       getnstr(last,31);
14       printw("Pleased to meet you, %s %s\n",
15               first,
16               last);
17       refresh();
18       getch();
19
20       endwin();
21       return(0);
22   }
```

A *refresh()* isn't required after the *getnstr()* functions at Lines 11 and 13; as with *getch()*, the *getnstr()* function automatically refreshes the screen.

Here is sample output:

```
First name: Dan
Last name: Gookin
Pleased to meet you, Dan Gookin
```

♦   *Though the* getnstr() *function does cap input, it's up to you (the programmer) to ensure that the value of* n *is less than the buffer size. Otherwise, input overflow occurs.*

SILENT INPUT

Like the *getch()* function, *getnstr()* is affected by various modifiers. For example, the *noecho()* function suppresses text output as it's typed.

08-08_urpwd.c

```
1    #include <ncurses.h>
2
3    int main()
4    {
5            char name[32];
6            char password[32];
7
8            initscr();
9
10           addstr("Name: ");
11           getnstr(name,32);
12           /* disable text output */
13           noecho();
14           addstr("Password: ");
15           getnstr(password,31);
16           /* enable text output */
17           echo();
18           printw("%s's password is '%s'\n",
19                   name,
20                   password);
21           refresh();
22           getch();
23
24           endwin();
25           return(0);
26    }
```

The *noecho()* function at Line 13 suppresses output as the user types a password (Line 15). Nothing appears on the screen.

FLUSHING INPUT

Ncurses text input is buffered, so the input functions read the buffer or test whether the buffer is empty. Buffering allows the user to type without having to wait for the program to catch up, and it prevents the requirement that the code constantly scan the keyboard.

To clear the buffer, use the *flushinp()* function:

```
flushinp()
```

After the above statement, the input buffer is cleared. The function returns OK on success, ERR otherwise.

You can use the *flushinp()* function to help clear the buffer of potentially unwanted keystrokes. For example, say your program is about to ask a very serious yes-or-no question. It's best to flush input at that point, to ensure that a lazy Y or undesired N isn't lurking in the buffer.

08-09_flush.c

```c
 1    #include <ncurses.h>
 2
 3    int main()
 4    {
 5        char buffer[81];
 6
 7        initscr();
 8
 9        addstr("Type. I'll wait...\n");
10        refresh();
11        napms(5000);              /* 5 seconds */
12
13        addstr("Flushing buffer.\n");
14        flushinp();
15        addstr("Here is what you typed:\n");
16        getnstr(buffer,80);
17
18        endwin();
19        return(0);
20    }
```

The program displays some text:

```
Type. I'll wait...
```

Type text, *la-di-da*. After a few seconds, you see:

```
Flushing buffer.
Here is what you typed:
```

The *flushinp()* function cleared (or flushed) all input, so no text appears.

9. Ncurses Windows

Ncurses is a windowed environment. These aren't the windows you see in a graphical operating system. Instead, they're a character array, displayed in a series of rows and columns on the terminal's screen. In Ncurses, you can deploy several windows, each with different dimensions and attributes.

Windows Prefix Functions

All Ncurses text output functions feature a window argument, targeting a specific window where characters appear. This rule holds true for the standard screen as well, though special pseudo functions (macros) are available that set `stdscr` as the window argument.

For example, the *addstr()* function is really the *waddstr()* function:

```
addstr("Text");
```

Expands to:

```
waddstr(stdscr,"Text");
```

The string `Text` is output to the standard screen at the cursor's location.

The first argument in a *w* (window) function is the name of a window variable, such as `stdscr` for the standard screen or the name of a window you created, as discussed in this chapter.

Not every window-specific function features the *w* prefix. For example, *getmaxyx()*, *getyx()*, *keypad()*, and *nodelay()*require a window variable as the first argument, but lack a *w* prefix:

```
getmaxyx(win,row,col)
```

```
getyx(win,y,x)
```

```
keypad(win,bf)
```

```
nodelay(win,bf)
```

In addition to the *w* prefix, many window-manipulating functions feature the *mv* prefix. This prefix indicates that the function requires a line and column argument along with other arguments.

When the *w* and *mv* prefixes are used together, the *mv* prefix comes first, yet the `win` argument comes before the `y` and `x` coordinate arguments. For example:

```
mvwaddch(stdscr,5,10,'Q');
```

Above, the letter Q is placed at position 5, 10 on the standard screen.

New Windows

All Ncurses programs feature the standard screen; the *initscr()* function creates it. You can create additional windows for output, as many as memory allows. To do so, you use the *newwin()* function:

```
newwin(rows,cols,y_org,x_org)
```

The arguments `rows` and `cols` set the window's size in characters, vertically and horizontally. The `y_org` and `x_org` arguments set the window's location on the standard screen, with coordinates 0, 0 as the upper left corner; `y_org` is the row and `x_org` is the column.

The range for all four arguments depends on screen size, as well as the system's memory.

The largest window can match the size of the standard screen.

The smallest is a one-character window.

Upon success, *newwin()* returns a pointer to a `WINDOW` structure. Use the `WINDOW` variable type to declare such a pointer in your code:

```
WINDOW *name;
```

This operation works like opening a file, where the `FILE` pointer is used. In Ncurses, the `WINDOW` variable is defined in `ncurses.h` and it references a structure that describes the window.

Upon failure, a `NULL` pointer is returned. The call fails because of a lack of memory, or that the window is too large or doesn't fit entirely on the screen.

To create a new window exactly the same size as the standard screen, specify all zeros in the *newwin()* call:

```
newwin(0,0,0,0);
```

New windows don't appear until they're refreshed. For this job,
use the *wrefresh()* function.

Yes, the *refresh()* function is actually a pseudo function, defined
as `wrefresh(stdscr)`. With a *wrefresh()* function, you must
specify the named window to make it visible.

POP-UP A NEW WINDOW

The following code creates a new window. The code includes
tests to ensure that the window is created and displays
appropriate messages one way or the other.

09-01_anotherwin.c

```
1    #include <ncurses.h>
2
3    int main()
4    {
5        WINDOW *another;
6
7        initscr();
8
9        addstr("This is the standard screen\n");
10       refresh();
11       getch();
12
13       /* create another window */
14       another = newwin(0,0,0,0);
15       if( another == NULL)
16       {
17           addstr("Unable to create window");
18           wrefresh();
19           getch();
20       }
21       else
22       {
23           waddstr(another,"This is another window");
24           wrefresh(another);
25           wgetch(another);
26       }
27
28       endwin();
29       return(0);
30   }
```

The WINDOW pointer variable `another` is created at line 5. The
newwin() function at Line 14 creates a window that matches the
size of the standard screen, and assigns its structure to pointer
`another`.

If the operation fails, the *if* test at line 15 passes, and the *addstr()* displays a message on the standard screen. Otherwise the *waddstr()* function in Line 23 outputs text to the new window, and the *wrefresh()* function at Line 24 updates and displays the window.

At Line 25, the *wgetch()* function reads input from the new window, `another`. See the later section, "Window Input Functions" for more details on *wgetch()*.

SWITCH WINDOWS

One of the points of having multiple windows is so that you can switch between them. It's the *wrefresh()* function that shuffles a window's contents to the front of the pile.

In the following code, the *bkgd()* function applies a different background to two windows, so that it's easier to tell which window is which. The *bkgd()* and text-color functions are introduced in Chapter 3.

09-02_switch.c

```
1    #include <ncurses.h>
2
3    int main()
4    {
5            WINDOW *second;
6
7            initscr();
8            start_color();
9
10           /* configure colors */
11           init_pair(1,COLOR_WHITE,COLOR_BLUE);
12           init_pair(2,COLOR_WHITE,COLOR_RED);
13
14           /* create the second window */
15           second = newwin(0,0,0,0);
16           if(second == NULL)
17           {
18                   endwin();
19                   puts("Unable to create window");
20                   return(1);
21           }
22           wbkgd(second,COLOR_PAIR(2));
23           waddstr(second,"This is the second window\n");
24
25           /* standard screen */
26           bkgd(COLOR_PAIR(1));
27           addstr("This is the standard screen\n");
28           addstr("Press Enter");
29           refresh();
30           getch();
```

```
31        /* show second window */
32        wrefresh(second);
33        getch();
34
35        endwin();
36        return(0);
37  }
```

The window `second` is created at Line 15. It's background color is set to white text on red at Line 22. Text is put to the `second` window at Line 23, but the window doesn't yet appear on the screen.

At Line 26, the standard screen's window is set to white text on a blue background. Text is put to the window in Lines 27 and 28. The *refresh()* function at Line 29 displays the window.

After the user presses a key (Line 30), the `second` window appears, thanks to the *wrefresh()* function at Line 32. Because of the different colors, it's visually obvious that a second window is viewed.

EXERCISE 09-03_SWITCHBACK.C

Modify the source code from `09-02_switch.c` so that after the second window is displayed, the user can press a key to again to view the standard screen. Keep reading in the next section to help you understand what's going on when you fail.

FORCE A REFRESH

If you attempted Exercise `09-03_switchback.c`, you probably noticed something: It didn't work. You may have added a *refresh()* function or even tried `wrefresh(stdscr)`. Either way, the standard screen didn't show up. This behavior isn't a bug, it's merely the way the *refresh()* function works, primarily to save time.

Internally, the *refresh()* function compares the window's buffer with a virtual screen buffer. The virtual screen buffer contains what Ncurses believes to be the current state of the terminal screen. Only differences between the two buffers are written to the screen. When both buffers are identical, the update is skipped.

In the case of Exercise `08-03_switchback.c`, the third *refresh()* call doesn't re-display the standard screen because that screen

87

hasn't changed. Therefore, the normal *refresh()* function doesn't do anything -- on purpose.

To force an update, use the *touchwin()* function:

```
touchwin(win)
```

The *touchwin()* function leads Ncurses to believe that every character in window **win** has been updated, or "touched," since the last *refresh()* call. The code shown in 09-04_touch.c provides the Exercise's proper solution.

09-04_touch.c

```
1    #include <ncurses.h>
2
3    int main()
4    {
5        WINDOW *second;
6
7        initscr();
8        start_color();
9
10       /* configure colors */
11       init_pair(1,COLOR_WHITE,COLOR_BLUE);
12       init_pair(2,COLOR_WHITE,COLOR_RED);
13
14       /* create the second window */
15       second = newwin(0,0,0,0);
16       if(second == NULL)
17       {
18           endwin();
19           puts("Unable to create window");
20           return(1);
21       }
22       wbkgd(second,COLOR_PAIR(2));
23       waddstr(second,"This is the second window\n");
24
25       /* standard screen */
26       bkgd(COLOR_PAIR(1));
27       addstr("This is the standard screen\n");
28       addstr("Press Enter");
29       refresh();
30       getch();
31       /* show second window */
32       wrefresh(second);
33       getch();
34       /* show standard screen again */
35       touchwin(stdscr);
36       refresh();
37       getch();
38
39       endwin();
40       return(0);
41   }
```

New code added between 09-02_switch.c and 09-04_touch.c is highlighted in green above.

WINDOWS OF A SMALLER SIZE

The largest size for a new window is the same size as the standard screen. The smallest size for a new window is a single character. In the following code, a window one-quarter the standard screen size is created.

09-05_halfpint.c

```
1    #include <ncurses.h>
2
3    int main()
4    {
5        WINDOW *tiny;
6
7        initscr();
8        start_color();
9
10       /* configure colors */
11       init_pair(1,COLOR_WHITE,COLOR_BLUE);
12       init_pair(2,COLOR_WHITE,COLOR_RED);
13
14       /* create the tiny window */
15       tiny = newwin(
16               LINES/2,
17               COLS/2,
18               LINES/4,
19               COLS/4);
20       if(!tiny)
21       {
22           endwin();
23           puts("Unable to create window");
24           return(1);
25       }
26       wbkgd(tiny,COLOR_PAIR(2));
27       waddstr(tiny,"This is a tiny window\n");
28
29       /* standard screen */
30       bkgd(COLOR_PAIR(1));
31       addstr("This is the standard screen\n");
32       addstr("Press Enter");
33       refresh();
34       getch();
35       /* show second window */
36       wrefresh(tiny);
37       getch();
38       /* show standard screen again */
39       touchwin(stdscr);
40       refresh();
41       getch();
42
43       endwin();
44       return(0);
```

```
45     |  }
```

This code is based on previous examples, save for Lines 15 through 19, where the *newwin()* command builds a window half the screen height and width. Constants `LINES` and `COLS` set the window size as well as position it in the center of the screen. I split the *newwin()* function across several lines so you can better see the math.

Beyond the new window's diminutive size, the rest of the code is identical to `09-04_touch.c`.

Upon running the program, you see the second window, `tiny`, appear with a red background overlaying the standard screen (blue background) window.

♦ *Re-size the terminal window (in the operating system's GUI) and re-run the program to ensure that the tiny window remains one-quarter size the terminal window.*

EXERCISE 09-06_QUAD.C

Write a program that places four windows on the screen, each a quarter size of the standard screen and positioned so that you can see all four windows at once. Color each window with a different background, such as red, green, blue, and cyan.

Window Input Functions

The *getch()* and *getnstr()* input function also have *w* prefix versions:

```
wgetch(win)
```

```
wgetnstr(win,buf,n)
```

Input is a keyboard thing and input works for your code whether you use *getch()* or *wgetch()* with a window argument. So why bother with a window argument?

The primary reason to assign keyboard input to a window is to specify input modification attributes. For example, the *keypad()*, *meta()*, *notimeout()*, and *timeout()* functions feature a window argument. When you use *wgetch()* or *wgetnstr()* on the same window with an attribute applied, you apply the modification to input. You can then use a different window to read input without the attribute applied.

♦   *You can read input from a specific window without having to refresh that window.*

Remove a Window

When you're done using a window, you use the *delwin()* function to release its WINDOW pointer variable:

```
delwin(win)
```

The *delwin()* function removes the window referenced by WINDOW pointer win. The window's contents remain on the screen after the call, but as the window no longer exists, you can't clear it or add new text.

09-07_twowin.c

```c
1    #include <ncurses.h>
2
3    int main()
4    {
5         WINDOW *one,*two;
6
7         initscr();
8
9         /* update the standard screen regardless */
10        refresh();
11        /* create two half-size windows */
12        one = newwin(LINES,COLS/2,0,0);
13        two = newwin(LINES,COLS/2,0,COLS/2);
14        if( one==NULL || two==NULL )
15        {
16             endwin();
17             puts("Unable to create windows");
18             return(1);
19        }
20
21        /* set backgrounds and text */
22        wbkgd(one,'|');
23        waddstr(one,"Window One\n");
24        wbkgd(two,'-');
25        waddstr(two,"Window Two\n");
26
27        /* update screen */
28        wrefresh(one);
29        getch();
30        wrefresh(two);
31        getch();
32
33        /* remove window 1 */
```

```
34        delwin(one);
35        waddstr(two,"Window one deleted\n");
36        wrefresh(two);
37        getch();
38
39        endwin();
40        return(0);
41    }
```

Two `WINDOW` pointers are created at Line 5, `one` and `two`.

Line 10 is important: The standard screen isn't used in this code, but it must be refreshed anyway. If not, the first window won't show up.

Lines 11 through 19 create the two windows, each of which are half the width of the standard screen.

Text and background are applied to each window in Lines 21 through 25.

In Lines 27 through 18, the windows are displayed, one at a time.

Finally, Line 34 removes window `one` and displays a message on window `two`. On the screen, the contents of window `two` remain.

♦ *The* delwin() *function cannot remove the standard screen,* `stdscr`. *To remove that window, use the* endwin() *function, which also terminates Ncurses.*

Window Borders

Ncurses features two functions to apply a border to a window:

`border()`

`box()`

See the descriptions elsewhere in this chapter for the argument lists, which can be quit long.

Both functions place text around the standard screen. The *border()* function also features a *w* prefix variation, *wborder()*, to apply the border to a named window. ACS line-drawing characters are used to create the border, or you can choose your own box-drawing characters.

The *box()* function is a simplified version of the *border()* function, having fewer arguments. It lacks a *w* prefix variation as a window argument is always required.

The border's characters aren't protected; they appear on the outside rows and columns of the window. To avoid overwriting the box, you must calculate a one-character offset for window-writing functions (or use a subwindow, covered in Chapter 10.)

THE STANDARD SCREEN BORDER

The format for the *border()* function is rather complex. It features eight arguments, one for each side and corner character used to draw the box. In its simplest format, the *border()* function is called with all zeros:

```
border(0,0,0,0,0,0,0,0);
```

The above statement places a single-line border around the standard screen.

If you prefer to specify your own characters to draw the border, they are in order:

- Left side character
- Right side character
- Top side character
- Bottom side character
- Top left corner character
- Top right corner character
- Bottom left corner character
- Bottom right corner character

When the terminal lacks access to ACS characters, ASCII characters approximating lines and corners are substituted.

09-08_border.c

```
1   #include <ncurses.h>
2
3   int main()
4   {
5       initscr();
6
7       border(0,0,0,0, 0,0,0,0);
8       move(1,1);
```

```
9              addstr("Now that's a swell border!\n");
10             refresh();
11             getch();
12
13             endwin();
14             return(0);
15     }
```

A single-line border is drawn around the edges of the standard screen, thanks to the eight zeros as arguments to the *border()* function in Line7.

A *move()* function at Line 8 ensures that the text displayed at line 9 appears within the window's border.

The newline ('\n'), added by *addstr()* in Line 9, wraps text to the next line, which erases to the end of the line. To fix the problem remove the newline character in the code.

◆ *Newlines ('\n') displayed in Ncurses erase to the end of the line, clobbering any text from the cursor to the right edge of the window.*

EXERCISE 09-09_ABORDER.C

Modify the code in `09-8_border.c` so that ASCII characters are used to create the border.

DRAW A BOX

Like the *border()* function, *box()* draws a line around a window. It has three arguments:

```
box(win,vert,horz)
```

The first argument is a window, which means if you want to box the standard screen, you must specify `stdscr`. The other two arguments are a vertical character and a horizontal character to draw the tops and sides, respectively. Or you can specify zero to use the default ACS line-drawing characters.

```
box(alpha,':','.');
```

The above statement draws a border around window `alpha`. The standard ASC corner characters are used for the corners, but for the vertical lines the ':' (colon) character is used. The '.' (period) appears for the horizontal lines.

In the following code sample, a single-line ACS character box is drawn around the standard screen.

09-10_box.c

```
1    #include <ncurses.h>
2
3    int main()
4    {
5            initscr();
6
7            box(stdscr,0,0);
8            refresh();
9            getch();
10
11           endwin();
12           return(0);
13    }
```

The *box()* function at Line 7 draws a border around the standard screen. This statement is equivalent to the *border()* function issued at Line 7 in the example code 09-08_border.c.

EXERCISE 09-11_QUADBORDERS.C

Take your solution for Exercise 09-06_quad.c and modify the code so that each window has a single-line border.

10. Subwindows

Much of the Ncurses' documentation on the Internet claims that subwindows are buggy and should be avoided. Yet, I believe they do have a useful place in your code. In my experience, I find a subwindow useful and a time-saver.

The Thing with Subwindows

Subwindows are like real windows in Ncurses in that they share the same data structure. You use the same `WINDOW` variable to create a subwindow as you do a full window. Ncurses functions that control or manipulate a window, also control and manipulate subwindows (with a few exceptions). But a subwindow is *not* the same thing as a real window. That's because a subwindow's memory is shared with its parent window.

For example, when you put a character to a subwindow, that character is also placed in the parent window.

The sticking point with a subwindow is that both it and its parent share the same data structure. So, in my mind, I prefer to think of a subwindow is merely as a convenient way to reference a specific portion of a parent window. Especially when you find yourself doing a lot of offset math and other calculations, creating a subwindow is a handy shortcut.

Create a Subwindow

Two functions create a subwindow, *subwin()* or *derwin()*:

`subwin(win,rows,cols,y,x)`

`derwin(win,rows,cols,y,x)`

The `win` argument represents the parent window, already created in your code.

The `rows` and `cols` arguments are the subwindow's height and width, respectively. These values much be less than the parent window's height and width.

The y and x arguments represent an offset, which is where the two functions differ: In the *subwin()* function, *y* and *x*, are coordinates relative to the standard screen; in the *derwin()* function, *y* and *x* are relative to the parent window.

After creation, the subwindow is addressed by using standard Ncurses output functions.

YOUR FIRST SUBWINDOW

When the *subwin()* or *derwin()* function is successful, a new window is created, returned as a WINDOW pointer. When the function fails, such as when no memory is available or the subwindow does not reside completely within the parent, NULL is returned.

The following code demonstrates the *subwin()* function. The subwindow is created on the standard screen.

10-01_sub1.c

```
1    #include <ncurses.h>
2
3    int main()
4    {
5    WINDOW *sub;
6
7            initscr();
8
9            /* create subwindow on stdscr */
10           sub = subwin(stdscr,LINES-2,COLS-2,1,1);
11           if( sub==NULL)
12           {
13                   endwin();
14                   puts("Unable to create subwindow");
15                   return(1);
16           }
17
18           /* draw a box around stdscr */
19           box(stdscr,0,0);
20           /* put text to the subwindow */
21           waddstr(sub,"I'm in a subwindow.\n");
22           refresh();
23           getch();
24
25           endwin();
26           return(0);
27    }
```

The subwindow is created in Line 10. It's exactly one row and column characters smaller than the standard screen and offset so that it rests one row and column inside the standard screen.

At Line 19, a box is drawn around the standard screen.

Line 21 places text inside the subwindow – but the text's newline doesn't erase the box around the standard window. That's because the text is specific to the subwindow. Yes, it also exists on the standard screen, the parent window, but it doesn't affect the parent window's box.

Only a single *refresh()* function is required at Line 22. It updates both the standard screen as well as its subwindow.

EXERCISE 10-02_SUB2.C

Crate a subwindow that's one quarter size the standard screen and place that subwindow in the center of its parent. Output text to both windows.

TEXT ACROSS WINDOWS

The following code demonstrates how subwindows share data with their parents. In the code, I use the *derwin()* function to create the subwindow, similar to what was done in example 10-01_sub1.c. The difference is that the *addstr()* function places the text on the standard screen, not in the subwindow directly.

10-03_sub3.c

```
1    #include <ncurses.h>
2
3    int main()
4    {
5    WINDOW *sub;
6
7        initscr();
8
9        /* create subwindow on stdscr */
10       sub = derwin(stdscr,LINES-2,COLS-2,1,1);
11       if( sub==NULL)
12       {
13           endwin();
14           puts("Unable to create subwindow");
15           return(1);
16       }
17
18       /* draw a box around stdscr */
19       box(stdscr,0,0);
20       /* put text to the stdscr */
21       addstr("I'm writing text\n");
22       addstr("to the standard screen.");
23       refresh();
24       getch();
25
```

```
26          wclear(sub);
27          wrefresh(sub);
28          getch();
29
30          endwin();
31          return(0);
32      }
```

The *derwin()* function creates a subwindow at Line 10. It's upper left corner location is set relative to the parent window, which is also the standard screen. So, effectively, it's identical to a program that would use *subwin()* to create the window.

Two strings are placed on the standard screen at Lines 21 and 22. As expected, these strings clobber the border set in Line 19.

The text placed on the standard screen is shared with the sub subwindow. Yet, when the *wclear()* function is used in Line 26, only the contents of the subwindow are erased.

The subwindow must be updated specifically, which is done in Line 27; because the standard screen window hasn't been "touched," the subwindow argument is required for a refresh.

Sub-Subwindows

Subwindows can have subwindows of their own, which is kind of crazy, but if you're using subwindows as offset, then an offset to an offset can be a useful thing.

10-04_subsub.c

```
1   #include <ncurses.h>
2
3   int main()
4   {
5       WINDOW *grandpa,*father,*son;
6       int gl,gc;
7
8       initscr();
9       refresh();  /* update stdscr */
10
11      /* set colors */
12      start_color();
13      init_pair(1,COLOR_WHITE,COLOR_BLUE);
14      init_pair(2,COLOR_RED,COLOR_YELLOW);
15      init_pair(3,COLOR_BLACK,COLOR_GREEN);
16
17      /* create windows */
18      grandpa = newwin(LINES-4,COLS-10,2,5);
19      getmaxyx(grandpa,gl,gc);
20      father = derwin(grandpa,gl/2,gc,gl/2,0);
```

```
21          son = derwin(father,gl/2,3,0,(gc-4)/2);
22
23          /* color windows and splash some text */
24          wbkgd(grandpa,COLOR_PAIR(1));
25          waddstr(grandpa,"I am Grandpa\n");
26          wbkgd(father,COLOR_PAIR(2));
27          waddstr(father,"I am Father\n");
28          wclrtobot(father);
29          wbkgd(son,COLOR_PAIR(3));
30          waddstr(son,"I am the boy\n");
31          wrefresh(grandpa);
32          getch();
33
34          endwin();
35          return(0);
36      }
```

To ensure that the windows show up, I added a *refresh()* function at Line 9. That's because this code doesn't use the standard screen, yet I've discovered in my travels that it's good practice to add a refresh of the standard screen before adding other windows.

The program creates three colorful windows: grandpa, which is a real window; father, which is a subwindow of grandpa; and son, which is a subwindow of father. All three windows share the same data.

Window father occupies the lower half of the grandpa window. The *derwin()* function is used to specify the offsets.

Subwindow son occupies the center column of the father subwindow, a column four-characters wide.

Background colors are applied to the windows in Lines 11 through 15. No error checking is done on the *start_color()* statement, nor is any error-checking done when the window and subwindows are created in Lines 17 through 21.

Offsets for the subwindows are calculated at Line 19, using the size of window grandpa. This calculation keeps the subwindows' locations and sizes relative to the parent window (grandpa) no matter what size the standard screen.

In Lines 23 through 29, color and text is added to each window. The background colors make the windows more dramatically visible on the screen.

Removing a Subwindow

The *delwin()* function removes the named window, whether it's a primary window or a subwindow:

```
delwin(win);
```

The `win` argument is the name of a `WINDOW` pointer variable, a subwindow.

As with a primary window, removing a subwindow doesn't remove its contents from the screen. Any text was written to the subwindow is inherited by the parent window, so nothing is truly lost.

10-05_delsub.c

```
1    #include <ncurses.h>
2
3    int main()
4    {
5         WINDOW *sub;
6         int x;
7
8         initscr();
9         start_color();
10        init_pair(1,COLOR_BLACK,COLOR_BLUE);
11
12        /* create subwindow */
13        sub=subwin(stdscr,LINES-10,COLS-10,4,5);
14        if( sub==NULL)
15        {
16             endwin();
17             puts("Unable to create subwindow");
18             return(1);
19        }
20
21        /* fill windows */
22        for(x=0;x<120;x++)
23             addstr("standard screen ");
24        wbkgd(sub,COLOR_PAIR(1));
25        for(x=0;x<200;x++)
26             waddstr(sub," sub ");
27        refresh();
28        wrefresh(sub);
29        getch();
30
31        /* delete subwindow */
32        delwin(sub);
33        mvaddstr(0,0,"Subwindow deleted ");
34        refresh();
35        getch();
36
37        endwin();
```

```
38              return(0);
39      }
```

By the time you see things (Line 28), the standard screen is filled with text and a blue-background subwindow appears in the center. Press the Enter key (Line 29), and then the *delwin()* function removes the subwindow.

The result is that the parent window (`stdscr`) inherits the subwindow's text. The *refresh()* at Line 24 doesn't remove the subwindow's contents.

♦ *Never remove a parent window that has active subwindows. Doing so results in ugly and unpredictable behavior.*

Subwindow Roundup

Subwindows work like real windows in many ways:

* Subwindows use a separate `WINDOW` data structure in memory

* Subwindows sport their own cursor, separate from the parent window's cursor.

* Subwindows can have their own color and text attributes.

* Subwindows are manipulated like regular windows, with a few exceptions.

A subwindow knows its parent, but parent windows are unaware of any subwindows. No error is triggered should you remove a window and not first remove its subwindows.

Finally, remember that subwindows share memory with their parent. Text written to a subwindow is also written to the parent. Likewise, the parent has no respect for its subwindow, and can effortlessly write over the subwindow's text. In fact, text written over the subwindow's text becomes part of the subwindow, thanks to the shared memory.

Chapter 20

11. Window Tricks: Copying and Moving

Windows aren't only containers for text and formatting. They're data structures. As such, you can copy text and attributes from one structure to another. You can duplicate windows. You can move windows.

Copy Window Contents

Ncurses features several window-copying functions:

`copywin()`

`overwrite()`

`overlay()`

`dupwin()`

Arguments for each function are presented later in this chapter. The differences between these functions are based on where and how the window is duplicated.

The *copywin()* function allows you the most control over what is copied and how it's pasted.

The *overwrite()* and *overlay()* functions are shortcuts for *copywin()*, which deal with overlapping parts of two windows.

The *dupwin()* function duplicates a window's data and structure to a new `WINDOW` variable.

ONE WINDOW OVERWRITES ANOTHER

The *overwrite()* function destructively copies text and attributes from one window to another:

`overwrite(swin,dwin)`

The two arguments are the source window `swin` and destination window `dwin`. Both windows must overlap for the function to work. If not, the function returns the `ERR` constant. (On success, `OK` is returned.)

11-01_overwrite1.c

```
1    #include <ncurses.h>
2
3    int main()
4    {
5        WINDOW *red,*blue;
6
7        initscr();
8        refresh();
9
10       /* colors */
11       start_color();
12       init_pair(1,COLOR_WHITE,COLOR_RED);
13       init_pair(2,COLOR_WHITE,COLOR_BLUE);
14
15       /* create windows */
16       red = newwin(10,20,2,22);
17       blue = newwin(10,20,5,32);
18       if( red==NULL || blue==NULL)
19       {
20           endwin();
21           puts("Unable to create windows");
22           return(1);
23       }
24
25       /* color and fill windows */
26       wbkgd(red,COLOR_PAIR(1) | 'r');
27       wbkgd(blue,COLOR_PAIR(2) | 'b');
28       wrefresh(red);
39       wrefresh(blue);
30       getch();
31
32       /* overwrite windows */
33       overwrite(red,blue);
34       wrefresh(blue);
35       getch();
36
37       endwin();
38       return(0);
39   }
```

This code creates two windows, red and blue. In Line 33, the *overwrite()* function copies a portion of window red to window blue, the portion that overlaps between them. The effect is that window red appears to be in front of window blue, but only the contents of that window are copied; the original contents of window blue are replaced.

The code in 11-01_overwrite.c doesn't do error-checking on the overwrite function. That's because I know the two windows overlap. If you create window blue at a new location, such as column 59, then the *overwrite()* function doesn't copy anything.

The function returns the ERR constant, but otherwise the code keeps going.

EXERCISE 11-02_OVERWRITE2.C

To prove that the contents of window red are copied to window blue, modify the source code 11-01_overwrite1.c so that the background on window red is changed to solid red after the *overwrite()* function (Line 33). Update both windows to prove that window red is clear but window blue still holds the copied text.

WHICH WINDOW IS ON TOP?

Copying window contents raises the issue of which window is "on top?" When multiple windows collect on the screen, the most recently-refreshed window appears on top or in front of the others. The *overwrite()* function clouds this issue, but if you change the order of the *wrefresh()* functions, you'll see how multiple windows can be shuffled.

OVERLAY INSTEAD OF OVERWRITE

The primary difference between the *overwrite()* and *overlay()* functions is that *overwrite()* is destructive; text in the target window is replaced by text from the source. With the *overlay()* function, text from the source window only fills in empty parts (spaces) in the destination window. Attributes are not copied.

11-03_overlay.c

```
1    #include <ncurses.h>
2
3    int main()
4    {
5        WINDOW *red,*blue;
6        int x;
7
8        initscr();
9        refresh();
10
11        /* colors */
12        start_color();
13        init_pair(1,COLOR_WHITE,COLOR_RED);
14        init_pair(2,COLOR_WHITE,COLOR_BLUE);
15
16        /* create windows */
17        red = newwin(10,24,2,22);
18        blue = newwin(10,24,5,32);
19        if( red==NULL || blue==NULL)
```

```
20              {
21                      endwin();
22                      puts("Unable to create windows");
23                      return(1);
24              }
25
26              /* color and fill windows */
27              wbkgd(red,COLOR_PAIR(1));
28              wbkgd(blue,COLOR_PAIR(2));
29              for(x=0;x<30;x++)
30              {
31                      waddstr(red,"o e l y ");
32                      waddstr(blue," r a   v");
33              }
34              wrefresh(red);
35              wrefresh(blue);
36              getch();
37
38              /* overlay windows */
39              overlay(red,blue);
40              wrefresh(blue);
41              getch();
42
43              endwin();
44              return(0);
45      }
```

Each window is filled with a different string, thanks to the *for* loop in Lines 29 through 33.

The *overlay()* function in Line 39 shares the same arguments as *overwrite()* in the earlier example, 11-01_overwrite1.c, but it behaves differently: When you run the program, you see two windows, the red one behind the blue one. Text from window red is then overlaid onto window blue. In the end, window blue holds the copied text; window red is unaffected.

As with the *overwrite()* function, the *overlay()* function affects only the overlapping portion of the windows.

THE MAGIC OF COPYWIN()

Both the *overwrite()* and *overlay()* functions are based on the complex *copywin()* function, which offers more control – and features a parade of arguments:

```
copywin(swin,dwin,srow,scol,drow,dcol,dxrow,dxcol
    ,type)
```

As with *overwrite()* and *overlay()*, the swin and dwin are WINDOW variables for the source and destination windows. Unlike those other two functions, these windows need not overlap.

The `srow` and `scol` arguments are the starting Y and X coordinates of the chunk of text to be copied from `swin` window.

The `drow` and `dcol` arguments are the Y and X coordinates where the window chunk will be copied into the `dwin` window.

Arguments `dxrow` and `dxcol` set the size of the chunk based on coordinates in the destination window `dwin`: `dxrow` is the bottom row and `dxcol` is the right-most column.

The *type* argument is either `TRUE` or `FALSE`. If `TRUE`, text copied non-destructively, like the *overlay()* function. When `type` is `FALSE`, text from the `swin` clobbers (overwrites) text in the `dwin` window.

11-04_copywin.c

```
1   #include <ncurses.h>
2
3   int main()
4   {
5       WINDOW *red,*blue;
6       int x;
7
8       initscr();
9       refresh();
10
11      /* colors */
12      start_color();
13      init_pair(1,COLOR_WHITE,COLOR_RED);
14      init_pair(2,COLOR_WHITE,COLOR_BLUE);
15
16      /* create windows */
17      red = newwin(10,24,5,10);
18      blue = newwin(10,24,5,40);
19      if( red==NULL || blue==NULL)
20      {
21          endwin();
22          puts("Unable to create windows");
23          return(1);
24      }
25
26      /* color and fill windows */
27      wbkgd(red,COLOR_PAIR(1));
28      wbkgd(blue,COLOR_PAIR(2));
29      for(x=0;x<34;x++)
30      {
31          waddstr(red,"red    ");
32          waddstr(blue,"   blue");
33      }
34      wrefresh(red);
35      wrefresh(blue);
36      getch();
37
38      /* copy window */
```

```
39              copywin(red,blue,0,0,1,4,5,10,TRUE);
40              wrefresh(blue);
41              getch();
42
43              endwin();
44              return(0);
45       }
```

The code in 11-04_copywin.c is similar to previous examples in this Chapter. The differences are that the two windows, red and blue, no longer overlap. Also, Line 39 contains the *copywin()* function:

```
copywin(red,blue,0,0,1,4,5,10,TRUE);
```

Here are the arguments:

red and blue are the WINDOW variables.

> 0,0 is the row (line) and column for the origin text to be copied from window red. These coordinates represent the upper left corner of the block.

> 1,3 are the upper left (row and column) coordinates where the block from window red will be pasted into window blue.

> 5,10 sets the lower right corner of the block relative to window blue; the block is 5 rows tall by 7 columns wide.

TRUE directs the *copywin()* function to non-destructively copy text into blank spaces in window blue.

When you run the code, you see the text redblue interspersed in window blue.

EXERCISE 11-05_CLOBBER.C

Modify Line 39 in 11-04_copywin.c so that the final argument is FALSE. Run the program to see a destructive copy from one window to the other.

PLAIN OLD WINDOW DUPLICATION

The final window copying function is *dupwin()*, which copies an entire window — size, text and all — to a new window, a duplicate. It's basically the *newwin()* function, but uses an existing window as a template to create a new window.

dupwin(win)

The *dupwin()* function returns a WINDOW pointer representing the new window.

11-06_dup.c

```
1    #include <ncurses.h>
2
3    int main()
4    {
5        WINDOW *fred,*barney;
6
7        initscr();
8        refresh();
9
10       /* Build window & wait */
11       fred = newwin(0,0,0,0);
12       waddstr(fred,"This is Fred.\n");
13       wrefresh(fred);
14       getch();
15
16       /* Create and show barney */
17       barney = dupwin(fred);
18       waddstr(barney,"This is Barney.\n");
19       wrefresh(barney);
20       getch();
21
22       /* Go back to fred */
23       waddstr(fred,"Nice to see you!\n");
24       wrefresh(fred);
25       getch();
26
27       /* One more time to barney */
28       waddstr(barney,"You too!\n");
29       touchwin(barney);
30       wrefresh(barney);
31       getch();
32
33       endwin();
34       return(0);
35   }
```

The new window barney is a duplicate of window fred, created in Line 17. Because fred already has text, barney inherits the text.

From Line 21 on, the two windows swap on the screen, though because the first line is identical, it might be difficult to track which window is which. At first you see:

This is Fred

You're looking at window fred, which is the same size as the standard screen. Press Enter.

```
This is Fred.
This is Barney
```

You're looking at window **barney**, which inherited text from window **fred**. Press Enter.

```
This is Fred.
Nice to see you!
```

This is window **fred** again; the text put to **barney** is covered up. Press Enter.

```
This is Fred.
This is Barney.
You too!
```

And the final screen is window **barney**.

If you don't use the *touchwin()* function at Line 29, then you don't see the text This is Barney on the last screen. That's because only the updated portion of window **barney** is displayed. The *touchwin()* function ensures that the entire window's contents appear.

The Moving Experience

When Ncurses creates a window, it doesn't really bolt it down on the screen. Just as you can change text within a window, text attributes, the cursor location, you can also change the window's position on the screen. To do so, use the *mvwin()* function:

```
mvwin(win,line,col)
```

The *mvwin()* function moves window **win** to new location **line**, **col**, relative to the standard screen, with location 0, 0 as the upper left corner. The only restriction is that the entire window must fit on the screen at the new location.

11-07_movewin.c

```
1    #include <ncurses.h>
2
3    int main()
4    {
5        WINDOW *alpha;
6
7        initscr();
8        refresh();
9
10       /* configure color */
11       start_color();
```

```
12              init_pair(1,COLOR_WHITE,COLOR_GREEN);
13
14              /* create window */
15              alpha = newwin(7,20,3,10);
16              if( alpha==NULL )
17              {
18                      endwin();
19                      puts("Unable to create window");
20                      return(1);
21              }
22
23              /* put text on alpha */
24              wbkgd(alpha,COLOR_PAIR(1));
25              mvwaddstr(alpha,1,2,"Window Alpha");
26              wrefresh(alpha);
27              getch();
28
29              /* move window alpha */
30              mvwin(alpha,10,43);
31              mvwaddstr(alpha,2,2,"Moved!");
32              wrefresh(alpha);
33              getch();
34
35              endwin();
36              return(0);
37      }
```

In this code, a new window **alpha** is crated at Line 15. It's splashed up on the screen and some text is added. All is good.

The *mvwin()* function at Line 30 relocates the window on the standard screen. All is not good. That's because the window now seems to be in two places at once. It's not, of course; the problem is that the standard screen must be touched and refreshed.

Add two lines to the code between Lines 31 and 32:

```
31+1            touchwin(stdscr);
31+2            refresh();
```

The standard screen requires a full touch because it hasn't changed since the initial *refresh()* at Line 8. The *touchwin()* function forces a full refresh, which erases the remnants of window

When using the *mvwin()* function, remember these points:

*   The window can be moved to any position where its full size is displayed on the screen. When one or more rows or columns falls off the edge of the screen, the window is not moved and the *mvwin()* function returns ERR.

* To complete the move, the window in the background must be updated. Use the *touchwin()* function to update the entire window, followed by a *refresh()* or *wrefresh()* function.

* Do not move subwindows. These windows share memory with their parent window and when you move the subwindow, Ncurses cannot update which text was moved in which window. (This is one of those Bad Things about subwindows.)

* Don't confuse the *mvwin()* function with *wmove()*. The former moves a window, the latter changes the cursor's location.

* It might be obvious, but I'll state it anyway: You cannot move the standard screen, `stdscr`.

12. Window Tricks: Wrapping and Scrolling

Text wrapping at the end of a line or text scrolling up a screen are expected behaviors: When the cursor arrives at the far-left column, the next character appears at the start of the following line. When text wanders of the lower right corner of the screen, everything scrolls up one line; the top line is removed and the bottom line is blank. This behavior is most likely based on paper through a teletype machine, the ancestor of all computer terminals, and why terminal interfaces use the letters TTY.

Wrapping text and scrolling lines on a screen don't just happen; software technology controls these behaviors work. Indeed, the technology is patented and royalties are earned based on these common and expected behaviors.

Text at the End of a Line

The natural behavior in Ncurses is that characters extending beyond the final (far right) column position wrap down to the next row. This effect holds for each row on the screen except for the last row. When scrolling is active for the window, then a character placed after the last row and column position scrolls the screen up one line.

12-01_scrolling1.c

```
1    #include <ncurses.h>
2
3    int main()
4    {
5         char text[] = "This is some wrapping. ";
6         int x;
7
8         initscr();
9
10        for(x=0;x<100;x++)
11        {
12             addstr(text);
13             napms(100);
14             refresh();
15        }
16        getch();
17
18        endwin();
```

```
19              return(0);
20          }
```

The string **text** defined at Line 5 is put to the standard screen 100 times at Line 12. The *napms()* function pauses, otherwise you wouldn't see text-wrapping in action. The screen doesn't scroll unless scrolling for the standard screen is enabled, as described in the next section.

Ncurses puts text to the screen one character at a time, advancing the cursor and wrapping text as necessary. Five exceptions exist for this rule:

Tabs. The tab character `'\t'` advances the cursor to the next tab stop. Default tab stops are set every 8 characters, though you can alter the global variable **TABSTOP** to reset the value.

Newline. The newline character `'\n'` drops the cursor position to the start of the next line. When the cursor is on the last row and scrolling is enabled for the window, the window scrolls up. Also, the newline character erases any existing text from the cursor's location to the end of the line.

Carriage Return. The carriage return character `'\r'` relocates the cursor to the first column (far left) on the current line.

Backspace. The backspace character `'\b'` decrements the cursor's column position, moving left one notch. This move is non-destructive; backspace doesn't backup and erase.

Control Characters. ASCII codes 1 through 31 and 127, exclusive of tab (9), newline (10), carriage return (13) and backspace (8) are displayed with caret notation, such as ^Q for code 17. Displaying these characters advances the cursor two positions.

Control code zero doesn't display anything. Most likely, it's interpreted as the null character, `'\0'`. (Traditionally, ^@ is the symbol for ASCII zero.) Code 127 displays as ^?.

Scroll Around

Scrolling is a window attribute, along with size, position, and background color. You can activate or deactivate scrolling, as well as manually scroll a window up or down by a given number of lines.

SCROLL THAT WINDOW!

A window's scrolling capability is disabled by default. You saw this lack of scrolling if you compiled and ran example code 12–01_scrolling1.c. To activate scrolling, use the *scrollok()* function:

```
scrollok(win,bf)
```

The `win` argument is a `WINDOW` variable representing a window on the screen, or `stdscr` for the standard screen. The `bf` argument is either `TRUE` or `FALSE` to activate or deactivate scrolling, respectively.

The following code adds a single line (highlighted in green) to the previous example, which enables scrolling for the standard screen:

12-02_scrolling2.c

```
1    #include <ncurses.h>
2
3    int main()
4    {
5        char text[] = "This is some wrapping. ";
6        int x;
7
8        initscr();
9
10       scrollok(stdscr,TRUE);
11       for(x=0;x<100;x++)
12       {
13           addstr(text);
14           napms(100);
15           refresh();
16       }
17       getch();
18
19       endwin();
20       return(0);
21   }
```

Text scrolled off the top of the screen is lost.

SCROLL A SUBWINDOW

Scrolling behavior isn't inherited by a subwindow from its parent window. The attribute must be set for each window.

12-03_scrollsub.c

```
1    #include <ncurses.h>
2
3    int main()
4    {
5            WINDOW *sub;
6            char text[] = "Scroll away! ";
7            int x;
8
9            initscr();
10
11           sub = subwin(stdscr,10,30,6,24);
12           scrollok(sub,TRUE);
13           for(x=0;x<35;x++)
14           {
15                   waddstr(sub,text);
16                   napms(50);
17                   wrefresh(sub);
18           }
19           getch();
20
21           endwin();
22           return(0);
23   }
```

This code has no error-checking on the *subwin()* function in Line 11. Remember to add checking to your own code, primarily to ensure that the subwindow fully lies within its parent.

The *scrollok()* function at Line 12 enables scrolling for the subwindow sub. Text is then put to the window, and only that portion of the screen scrolls.

MANUAL SCROLLING

The *scroll()* function manually scrolls text on a window where scrolling is enabled:

```
scroll(win)
```

The win argument is the name of a WINDOW variable. That window scrolls up one line of text.

12-04_scroll.c

```
1    #include <ncurses.h>
2
3    int main()
```

```
4     {
5           int y;
6
7           initscr();
8
9           /* enable scrolling */
10          scrollok(stdscr,TRUE);
11
12          /* place junk on the screen */
13          for(y=0;y<LINES;y++)
14                  mvprintw(y,0,"%2d",y);
15          refresh();
16          getch();
17
18          /* scroll up one line */
19          scroll(stdscr);
20          refresh();
21          getch();
22
23          endwin();
24          return(0);
25    }
```

Scrolling is enabled for the standard screen at Line 10. Lines 12 through 15 fill the screen with some text. Finally, the *scroll()* function at Line 19 cranks every row of text up a notch, creating a blank row at the bottom.

Here are some things to notice when the screen scrolls:

* The top line of the window is scrolled away; it disappears.

* All lines after the top line are each scrolled up one notch

* A blank line fills the last line of the screen

* The cursor position *does not* change; it remains at the same coordinates as before the scroll. So, if the cursor is at position 10,15, it won't scroll up to line 9,15, but remains at 10,15.

SCROLL BY LEAPS AND BOUNDS

Rather than issue multiple *scroll()* functions, you can instead use the *scrl()* function.

```
scrl(n)
```

The *scrl()* function scrolls the standard screen *n* number of lines. To scroll up three lines, n would be 3. To make *scrl()* imitate the *scroll()* function, use `scrl(1)`.

12-05_scrup3.c

```
1    #include <ncurses.h>
2
3    int main()
4    {
5        int y;
6
7        initscr();
8
9        scrollok(stdscr,TRUE);
10       for(y=0;y<=LINES;y++)
11           mvprintw(y,0,"Line %d",y);
12       refresh();
13       getch();
14
15       scrl(3);
16       refresh();
17       getch();
18
19       endwin();
20       return(0);
21   }
```

The *scrl()* function in Line 15 hops text three rows up the screen. Blank rows replace the rows scrolled up from the bottom. As with the *scroll()* function, the cursor's position on the screen is unaffected by the *scrl()* function.

The full version of the *scrl()* function is *wscrl()*, which includes a window argument:

```
wscrl(win,n)
```

Window `win` must have its scrolling attribute set, otherwise the *wscrl()* function returns the ERR constant.

♦ *Internally,* wscrl() *is the only scrolling function;* scroll() *is a macro or pseudo function that calls the* wscrl() *function with an argument of 1.*

NEGATIVE SCROLLING

The *scrl()* function's n argument can be a negative value, in which case lines are scrolled down the screen, not up.

When text in a window is scrolled down, blank lines appear at the top. Text at the bottom of the screen is scrolled into oblivion. The cursor's position is unchanged.

SCROLL A REGION

Window scrolling affects all rows of text in the window. You can use the *setscrreg()* function to set the scrolling region of a window, narrowing the scroll effect to a smaller clutch of rows.

```
setscrreg(top,bottom)
```

The `top` argument is the top row for the scrolling region, with 0 representing the top row on the window. The `bottom` argument is the bottom row of the scrolling region. By default, both values are set to the top row and bottom row of the window. The `top` value must be less than the `bottom` value.

To make the *setscrreg()* function work, you must first enable scrolling (use the *scrollok()* function) and then use an *scrl()* function (or the *scroll()* function) to manipulate text within the scrolling region.

12-06_scrollreg.c

```
1    #include <ncurses.h>
2
3    int main()
4    {
5            char text[] = "Scroll me! ";
6            int x;
7
8            initscr();
9
10           bkgd('.');
11           scrollok(stdscr,TRUE);
12           setscrreg(3,LINES-3);
13
14           for(x=0;x<200;x++)
15           {
16                   addstr(text);
17                   napms(25);
18                   refresh();
19           }
20           getch();
21
22           endwin();
23           return(0);
24    }
```

The standard screen background is set to a series of dots in line 10. Scrolling is enabled in Line 11, and the scrolling region is set to line 4 and the third line from the bottom of the screen in Line 12.

As text output reaches the bottom of the screen, only the center portion of the window scrolls; the top and bottom remain static.

The *wsetscrreg()* function is the window-specific version of the *setscrreg()* function. Its format is:

```
wsetscrreg(win,top,bottom
```

13. Pads

The point of a window in Ncurses is to present information on the screen. Occasionally, you may desire to have that information prepared, but not presented. One way to accomplish that task is to not refresh a window. A better way is to create a pad.

Pads are window data structures. Unlike a window, they aren't limited in size by the terminal's screen proportions. You can make a pad as big as memory allows. You can output text to the pad, which works just like window output., but you can choose which part of the pad to display, or copy, to the standard screen.

The Pad Window Data Structure

Pads are like windows with regards to their creation, text output, and display. They use the same WINDOW pointer, and many of the same window functions. The two differences are in the function that creates the pad and the function that refreshes or outputs the pad's contents to the standard screen.

And, yes, pads output only to the standard screen.

HELLO, PAD

The *newpad()* function creates a pad, which is a storage area of a given size in rows and columns:

```
newpad(rows,cols)
```

rows and cols set the height and width of the pad in characters. Values range from 1 up to whatever memory can handle. If the pad is too large, a NULL pointer is returned.

The value returned from newpad() is the address of a WINDOW structure in memory, just like a regular window.

13-01_newpad1.c

```
1    #include <ncurses.h>
2
3    int main()
4    {
5        WINDOW *p;
6
7        initscr();
```

```
 8
 9                    /* create a new pad */
10                    p = newpad(50,100);
11                    if( p==NULL )
12                    {
13                            endwin();
14                            puts("Unable to create pad");
15                            return(1);
16                    }
17
18                    addstr("New pad created");
19                    refresh();
20                    getch();
21
22                    endwin();
23                    return(0);
24            }
```

The new pad p is created at Line 10. Lines 11 through 16 confirm that the pad exists. Text confirming its creation is displayed to the standard screen in Line 18.

This code doesn't output any text to the pad or do anything else to the pad, other than create it.

DISPLAY PAD CONTENTS

To add text to a pad, you use Ncurses' text-output functions, specifying the pad's WINDOW variable name as the window argument. You might suspect that the next step is to *refresh()* the pad so that the contents are visible – but not so fast.

First, the *prefresh()* function is used instead of *refresh()* or *wrefresh()*:

```
prefresh(pad,pminrow,pmincol,sminrow,smincol,smax
        row,smaxcol)
```

The *prefresh()* function requires origin and output coordinates. These specify which chunk of data from the pad to display and at which specific location to put the text on the standard screen. Effectively, the function copies a rectangular chunk of text from the pad to the standard screen.

The upper left coordinates of the chunk on the pad are set by the pminrow and pmincol arguments (think *p* for *pad*).

The sminrow and smincol arguments set the upper left corner for the rectangle on the standard screen (think *s* for *standard screen*). Then the smaxrow and smaxcol define the size of the rectangle as measured from the standard screen's original, coordinates 0, 0.

The arguments `smaxrow` and `smaxcol` must be greater than `sminrow` and `smincol`, respectively, and they must be located on the standard screen. Though the pad can be larger than the standard screen, the chunk displayed must fit within the screen's dimensions.

13-02_newpad2.c

```
1    #include <ncurses.h>
2
3    int main()
4    {
5        WINDOW *p;
6        int x;
7
8        initscr();
9
10       /* create a new pad */
11       p = newpad(50,100);
12       if( p==NULL )
13       {
14           endwin();
15           puts("Unable to create pad");
16           return(1);
17       }
18
19       /* fill the pad */
20       for(x=0;x<500;x++)
21           wprintw(p,"%4d",x);
22
23       addstr("Press Enter to update");
24       refresh();
25       getch();
26
27       prefresh(p,0,0,5,5,16,45);
28       getch();
29
30       endwin();
31       return(0);
32   }
```

This code is based on 13-01_newpad1.c, with new and changed lines highlighted in green.

Lines 19 through 21 fill the pad with numbers, just some text.

The *prefersh()* function in Line 27 copies a chunk of text from the pad to a rectangle on the standard screen. This function automatically updates (refreshes) the standard screen, so a *refresh()* statement is redundant.

125

Subpads

Just as windows can have subwindows, pads can sport subpads. The subpad shares memory with the parent; changing the contents of a subpad changes the text on a pad.

As with my subwindow philosophy, the subpad works best as an offset reference to the pad. So, if you're working on a certain part of the pad, you can quickly create a subpad to avoid tedious math calculations.

To create a subpad, you must first create a pad. Then use the *subpad()* function:

```
subpad(p,rows,cols,y,x)
```

p is the parent pad. rows and cols set the subpad's size, which (logically) cannot be greater than the parent's size. y and x set the subpad's position relative to the parent, where 0,0 is the upper left corner.

When the *subpad()* call is successful, a subpad is created in memory and a pointer to a WINDOW structure is returned, otherwise NULL is returned.

13-03_sonofpad.c

```
1    #include <ncurses.h>
2
3    int main()
4    {
5         WINDOW *pop,*son;
6         int x;
7
8         initscr();
9
10        /* create a new pad */
11        pop = newpad(50,50);
12        if( pop==NULL )
13        {
14             endwin();
15             puts("Unable to create pad");
16             return(1);
17        }
18
19        /* fill the pad */
20        for(x=0;x<50;x++)
21             waddstr(pop,"Hello ");
22
23        /* create the subpad */
24        son = subpad(pop,10,10,0,0);
```

```
25              if( son==NULL)
26              {
27                      endwin();
28                      puts("Unable to create subpad");
29                      return(1);
30              }
31
32              addstr("Press Enter to update");
33              refresh();
34              getch();
35
36              prefresh(son,0,0,5,5,15,15);
37              getch();
38
39              endwin();
40              return(0);
41      }
```

The subpad is created at Line 24. It's set at a size 10 lines by 10 columns at offset 0, 0 of the pad pop.

The *prefresh()* function at Line 36 splashes the son pad to the standard screen.

In this example, nothing spectacular happens. Again, a subpad (like a subwindow) is best for accessing text at specific offsets within its parent pad.

Pad Miscellany

You probably won't use pads that much. I've used them as a buffer. For example, I've loaded a long text file into a pad. Then I *prefresh()* chunks of that text to the standard screen to display help text. Beyond that, I've not used pads. I've never used a subpad.

REMOVE A PAD

Pads are blown to smithereens just like windows. The same function is used, *delwin()*:

```
delwin(pad)
```

The above function returns OK when the named pad is successfully removed or it returns ERR when something untoward happens.

The *delwin()* function also removes subpads. As with subwindows, ensure that you remove the subpad *before* you remove its parent pad.

FORBIDDEN PAD STUFF

The following window functions cannot be used with a pad:

mvwin()

scroll()

scrl()

subwin()

wrefresh()

wnoutrefresh()

14. Mouse Input

Ncurses can interface with a mouse or similar pointing device attached to a computer, even a mouse hovering in a terminal window. The mouse's pointer position and its button conditions are read as input; mouse movement isn't monitored.

Hello, Mouse

Two tests must be made before you can code a program that reads mouse input:

1. You must confirm that Ncurses has the smarts to read the mouse.

2. You must determine whether the terminal window can communicate mouse information.

For the first test, check constant value `NCURSES_MOUSE_VERSION`. If it's greater than zero, Ncurses can read mouse input.

For the second text, use the *mousemask()* function:

```
mousemask(newmask,*oldmask)
```

The `newmask` argument tells Ncurses which mouse events to trap. It's a variable of the *mmask_t* type, though constants are used that represent mouse events. These constants are defined in `ncurses.h`, and listed in Table 14-1.

MOUSE ACTION CONSTANT	VALUE
BUTTON1_RELEASED	0x00000001
BUTTON1_PRESSED	0x00000002
BUTTON1_CLICKED	0x00000004
BUTTON1_DOUBLE_CLICKED	0x00000008
BUTTON1_TRIPLE_CLICKED	0x00000010
BUTTON1_RESERVED_EVENT	0x00000020
BUTTON2_RELEASED	0x00000040

BUTTON2_PRESSED	0x00000080
BUTTON2_CLICKED	0x00000100
BUTTON2_DOUBLE_CLICKED	0x00000200
BUTTON2_TRIPLE_CLICKED	0x00000400
BUTTON2_RESERVED_EVENT	0x00000800
BUTTON3_RELEASED	0x00001000
BUTTON3_PRESSED	0x00002000
BUTTON3_CLICKED	0x00004000
BUTTON3_DOUBLE_CLICKED	0x00008000
BUTTON3_TRIPLE_CLICKED	0x00010000
BUTTON3_RESERVED_EVENT	0x00020000
BUTTON4_RELEASED	0x00040000
BUTTON4_PRESSED	0x00080000
BUTTON4_CLICKED	0x00100000
BUTTON4_DOUBLE_CLICKED	0x00200000
BUTTON4_TRIPLE_CLICKED	0x00400000
BUTTON4_RESERVED_EVENT	0x00800000
BUTTON_CTRL	0x01000000
BUTTON_SHIFT	0x02000000
BUTTON_ALT	0x04000000
ALL_MOUSE_EVENTS	0x07FFFFF
REPORT_MOUSE_POSITION	0x08000000

Table 14-1: Mouse action constants and values.

The best constant to use in the *mousemask()* function is
ALL_MOUSE_EVENTS, which tells Ncurses to keep an eye on
every mouse button, up or down, clicked, double- or triple-
clicked, or used in combination with Shift, Alt, or Ctrl keys.

The second argument in *mousemask()* is *oldmask*. It's also a
mmask_t variable representing the value returned from a

previous *mousemask()* function, though NULL is specified most of the time.

14-01_mousetest.c

```
1    #include <ncurses.h>
2
3    int main()
4    {
5            initscr();
6
7            if( NCURSES_MOUSE_VERSION>0)
8            {
9                    addstr("Mouse functions available.\n");
10                   mousemask(ALL_MOUSE_EVENTS,NULL);
11                   addstr("Mouse Active");
12           }
13           else
14           {
15                   addstr("Mouse functions unavailable.\n");
16           }
17           refresh();
18           getch();
19
20           endwin();
21           return(0);
22    }
```

This code determines whether Ncurses has mouse functions available at Line 7. If so, the mouse is enabled at Line 10, though no code reads the mouse's position or status.

Appropriate text is displayed depending on the value of the NCURSES_MOUSE_VERSION constant.

◆   *One of the reasons your terminal might not pass on mouse functions is that the operating system intercepts them first. If possible, disable mouse selection functions for the terminal window.*

Read the Mouse

After *mousemask()* initializes the mouse, and tells Ncurses which mouse events to scan, you use two functions to read the mouse:

getch()

getmouse(&musevent)

Just as the *getch()* function reads the keyboard, it also detects mouse input. Mouse input is defined as the KEY_MOUSE character. You must use *keypad()* function activate extended keyboard reading for *getch()* to detect KEY_MOUSE. Further, many programmers add the *noecho()* function so that *getch()* doesn't display stray text while the mouse is read.

After *getch()* indicates mouse activity, use the *getmouse()* function to retrieve information about the event:

`getmouse(&musevent)`

`musevent` is a variable of the `MEVENT` type:

`MEVENT musevent;`

You pass the `MEVENT` variable to the *getmouse()* function as a pointer, so if the variable isn't declared as a pointer, prefix the `&` (ampersand) to fetch its address.

`getmouse(&musevent);`

After the *getmouse()* function, review the `MEVENT` structure's members to determine what happened where. The structure's members are described in Table 14-2.

MEMBER	MOUSE EVENT
`id`	Unique ID number (to distinguish between multiple input devices)
`x`	Screen column coordinate
`y`	Screen row coordinate
`z`	Undefined
`bstate`	Bit pattern representing mouse button action

Table 14-2: Events recorded in the MEVENT structure.

Here is a summary of steps needed to read a mouse event:

* Issue the *noecho()* and *keypad()* functions to prepare *getch()* for reading mouse events.

* Issue the *mousemask()* function to tell Ncurses which mouse events to track.

* Compare *getch()* input with `KEY_MOUSE` to see whether a mouse event has occurred.

* Upon finding `KEY_MOUSE` input, use *getmouse()* to read the event's information into an `MEVENT` structure.

      *   Examine the MEVENT structure's members to determine what event took place at which coordinates on the screen.

WHERE DID YOU CLICK THAT MOUSE?

The following code reads information about where the mouse was clicked and displays those coordinates on the screen.

14-02_mspy.c

```
1    #include <ncurses.h>
2
3    int main()
4    {
5         MEVENT mort;
6         int ch;
7
8         initscr();
9         noecho();
10        keypad(stdscr,TRUE);
11
12        mousemask(ALL_MOUSE_EVENTS,NULL);
13        while(1)
14        {
15             ch = getch();
16             if( ch == KEY_MOUSE )
17             {
18                  getmouse(&mort);
19                  move(0,0);
20                  clrtoeol();
21                  printw("%d\t%d",mort.y,mort.x);
22                  refresh();
24                  continue;
25             }
26             if( ch == '\n' )
27                  break;
28        }
29
29        endwin();
30        return(0);
31   }
```

This code doesn't check to ensure that Ncurses mouse functions are available or that the terminal is ready to cough up mouse details. Refer to the earlier code 14-01_mousetest.c for an example.

The code configures the mouse for input in Line 9, 10, and 12. Line 15 uses the *getch()* function to read the keyboard and mouse. If KEY_MOUSE input is found, the y (row) and x (column) coordinates are displayed.

The program runs until the user presses the Enter key (Line 26).

♦   *If the program fails to read the mouse, ensure that the terminal window doesn't intercept mouse input for text-selection. Even so, not every terminal window reads mouse input.*

EXERCISE 14-03_CLICKPUT.C

Write code that places an asterisk at the mouse click location on the screen.

WHAT CLICKED?

The following code uses the predefined button constants to display information about which mouse button was pressed.

14-04_bclick.c

```
 1    #include <ncurses.h>
 2
 3    int main(void)
 4    {
 5        MEVENT mort;
 6        int ch;
 7
 8        initscr();
 9        noecho();
10        keypad(stdscr,TRUE);
11
12        mousemask(ALL_MOUSE_EVENTS,NULL);
13
14        while(1)
15        {
16            ch = getch();
17            if( ch == KEY_MOUSE )
18            {
19                clear();
20                getmouse(&mort);
21                switch(mort.bstate)
22                {
23                case BUTTON1_PRESSED:
24                    mvaddstr(0,0,"B1 Press");
25                    break;
26                case BUTTON1_RELEASED:
27                    mvaddstr(1,0,"B1 Release");
28                    break;
29                case BUTTON1_CLICKED:
30                    mvaddstr(2,0,"B1 Click");
31                    break;
32                case BUTTON1_DOUBLE_CLICKED:
33                    mvaddstr(3,0,"B1 2xClick");
34                    break;
35                case BUTTON2_PRESSED:
36                    mvaddstr(0,20,"B2 Press");
37                    break;
38                case BUTTON2_RELEASED:
```

```
39                          mvaddstr(1,20,"B2 Release");
40                          break;
41                      case BUTTON2_CLICKED:
42                          mvaddstr(2,20,"B2 Click");
43                          break;
44                      case BUTTON2_DOUBLE_CLICKED:
45                          mvaddstr(3,40,"B2 2xClick");
46                          break;
47                      case BUTTON3_PRESSED:
48                          mvaddstr(0,40,"B3 Press");
49                          break;
50                      case BUTTON3_RELEASED:
51                          mvaddstr(1,40,"B3 Release");
52                          break;
53                      case BUTTON3_CLICKED:
54                          mvaddstr(2,40,"B3 Click");
55                          break;
56                      case BUTTON3_DOUBLE_CLICKED:
57                          mvaddstr(3,40,"B3 2xClick");
58                          break;
59                      default:
60                          break;
61                  }
62                  refresh();
63                  continue;
64              }
65          if( ch == '\n' )
66              break;
67          }
68
69      endwin();
70      return 0;
71  }
```

When you run the code, remember to press and hold the mouse button, then release. You'll see the **Press** and **Release** text appear on the screen. Also, click and double click to see that output.

It surprised me that the right mouse button was read as B3 by the code. The wheel button was read as B2.

Refer to Table 14-1 for the full list of mouse events.

15. Miscellany

This eBook covers many of the basic Ncurses functions, yet it only scratches the surface. To wrap things up, I've collected a few additional functions and tossed them into this final chapter.

Hide the Cursor

Sometimes the blinking (or not) cursor is a benefit, sometimes it just gets in the way. The *curs_set()* function lets you disable the cursor, hiding it from view:

```
curs_set(n)
```

The value of n can be 0, 1, or 2:

>0 makes the cursor invisible

>1 sets the cursor to normal mode

>2 sets the cursor to a *very* visible mode.

Not every terminal supports the *curs_set()* function. If ERR is returned, the function does nothing. Otherwise, you can run the following code to see the effect:

15-01_cursset.c

```
1    #include <ncurses.h>
2
3    int main()
4    {
5        initscr();
6
7    /* first, turn the cursor off */
8        curs_set(0);
9        addstr("  <- The cursor has been turned off");
10       move(0,0);
11       refresh();
12       getch();
13
14   /* second, turn the cursor on */
15       curs_set(1);
16       addstr("\n  <- The cursor now on");
17       move(1,0);
18       refresh();
19       getch();
20
21   /* third, turn the cursor very on */
22       curs_set(2);
23       addstr("\n  <- The cursor is now very on");
```

```
24          move(2,0);
25          refresh();
26          getch();
27
28          endwin();
29          return(0);
30      }
```

Line Drawing

Chapter 9 covered the *box()* and *border()* functions, which are specific to a window. To draw other lines, you can access alternative character set characters, use Unicode, or employ these functions:

`hline(ch,n)`

`vline(ch,n)`

The *hline()* and *vline()* functions draw a horizontal or vertical line from the cursor's current position right or down, respectively. The line is drawn by using character `ch`. When `ch` isn't specified, one of the standard line drawing character is used instead. Argument `n` sets the length of the line in characters.

Both functions draw the line from the cursor's current position. Neither function alters the cursor's position.

15-02_steps.c

```
1       #include <ncurses.h>
2
3       int main()
4       {
5           int y,x,maxy,maxx;
6
7           initscr();
8
9           getmaxyx(stdscr,maxy,maxx);
10
11          for(y=x=0;y<maxy;y++,x+=2)
12          {
13              move(y,x);
14              hline(0,maxx-x);
15              vline(0,maxy-y);
16          }
17          refresh();
18          getchar();
19
20          endwin();
21          return(0);
22      }
```

This program's output shows a cascade of vertical and horizontal lines with an origin in the upper left corner of the screen.

You can save time by combining the cursor's location (Y and X positions) with the *hline()* and *vline()* functions. The variations are *mvhline()* and *mvvlin()*. A *w* prefix can also be added to send output to a specific window.

EXERCISE 15-03_PLUS.C

Code a program that uses the *hline()* and *vline()* functions to display a plus (+) on the standard screen. You get bonus points if it's a hollow plus and not just two lines that intersect.

Save the Screen

As a data structure, it's possible to save an Ncurses window to a file. Further, you can load a saved Ncurses data structure into a window. The quartet of functions that handle the task are:

```
scr_dump(*filename)

scr_restore(*filename)

putwin(win,*FILE)

getwin(win,*FILE)
```

The *scr_dump()* and *putwin()* functions write information from the current screen or a specific window to the named file, respectively.

The *scr_restore()* and *getwin()* functions read information from a file back into the current screen or a named window, respectively

For the *scr_dump()* and *scr_restore()* functions, the `filename` argument is a string, a filename. It is not a `FILE` handle. These functions open, read, and close the named file; you do need to *fopen()* or *fclose()* the file.

The *putwin()* and *getwin()* function sport a window argument, `win`, which is the name of the `WINDOW` pointer referencing the window to be saved or restored. The `FILE` argument is a file handle pointer returned from an *fopen()* function.

The *scr* functions are the "screen shot" functions; they work with the current screen, what you see in the terminal window. The contents saved or restored could be a collection of visible windows or a single window. The *scr_dump()* function saves the current screen's contents to the named file; the *scr_restore()* function retrieves previously-saved screen contents, placing the data back on the current screen.

The *putwin()* and *getwin()* functions work with a window, not the current screen. That window could also be the standard screen.

The *scr_dump()* and *putwin()* functions overwrite any existing file.

When the dump or restore is successful, the functions return OK, otherwise ERR is returned.

TAKE A SCREEN DUMP

The following code displays the standard screen as well as a window, **w**. the *scr_dump()* function captures the current screen, saving it to a file named dump.win.

The *scr_dump()* function performs what old timers refer to as a "screen dump." The inelegant term "dump" simply means to transfer a chunk of (often raw) data from one device to another. In the case of a screen dump, the data from the screen is saved to a file.

15-04_dumpwin.c

```
1    #include <ncurses.h>
2    #include <stdlib.h>
3    #include <time.h>
4
5    int main()
6    {
7            char word[7];
8            int x,w,r;
9
10           srandom((unsigned)time(NULL));
11           word[6] = '\0';
12           initscr();
13
14    /* add some random 6-char words */
15           for(x=0;x<200;x++)
16           {
17                   for(w=0;w<6;w++)
18                           word[w] = (random() % 26) + 'a';
19                   printw("%s\t",word);
20           }
21           addstr("\n Press Enter to dump the screen ");
```

```
22          refresh();
23          getch();
24
25   /* write the window */
26          r = scr_dump("dump.win");
27          if( r == ERR)
28                  addstr("Error writing window");
29          else
30                  addstr("File written; press Enter");
31          refresh();
32          getch();
33
34          endwin();
35          return(0);
36   }
```

Lines 14 through 23 work to write 200 random words to the screen. The result is something unique on the screen. The *scr_dump()* function is issued at Line 26, with its result tested at Line 27. If the function fails, ERR is returned, otherwise the file is written.

RESTORE THE SCREEN

The *scr_restore()* function reads a screen dump from a file into memory, directly to the standard screen. Only the filename is required as an argument.

15-05_undump.c

```
1    #include <ncurses.h>
2
3    int main()
4    {
5           int r;
6
7           initscr();
8
9           addstr("Press Enter to restore the screen");
10          refresh();
11          getch();
12
13   /* restore the window */
14          r = scr_restore("dump.win");
15          if( r == ERR)
16                  addstr("Error reading window file ");
17          refresh();
18          getch();
19
20          endwin();
21          return(0);
22   }
```

The screen previously saved in the file dump.win by code 15-05_dumpwin.c is restored to the screen. The *scr_restore()* function at Line 14 does all the heavy lifting.

DUMP A WINDOW

The *putwin()* function writes the contents of a window to a file. It's the same type of data saved for the *scr_dump()* function, but instead of the current screen, only data from the named window is saved.

When the contents of a window must be save to disk, use the *putwin()* and *getwin()* functions:

```
putwin(win,file)

win = getwin(file)
```

In both functions, win is the name of a WINDOW pointer, indicated some window created in Curses. file is a FILE pointer representing an open file. Use the *fopen()* function to open the file. Use the *fclose()* function when you're done to close the file.

15-06_wputfile.c

```
1    #include <ncurses.h>
2
3    int main()
4    {
5            FILE *wfile;
6            WINDOW *win;
7            int r;
8
9            initscr();
10           start_color();
11           init_pair(1,COLOR_WHITE,COLOR_BLUE);
12           refresh();
13
14   /* Crete and show window */
15           win = newwin(3,10,7,30);
16           wbkgd(win,COLOR_PAIR(1));
17           box(win,0,0);
18           mvwaddstr(win,1,2,"Window");
19           wrefresh(win);
20           getch();
21
22   /* open file */
23           wfile = fopen("window.win","w");
24           if( wfile==NULL )
25           {
26                   endwin();
27                   puts("File creation error");
28                   return(1);
```

```
29                    }
30
31          /* write window data */
32                  r = putwin(win,wfile);
33                  fclose(wfile);
34                  addstr("Window data written");
35                  refresh();
36                  getch();
37
38                  endwin();
39                  return(0);
40          }
```

Lines 14 through 20 set a tiny blue window on the screen.

In Line 23, a file is opened; error handing is done on Line 24 through 29.

At Line 32, the *putwin()* function writes the tiny window's data to a file, `window.win`. The following code reads that file and displays the window saved:

15-07_wgetfile.c

```
1    #include <ncurses.h>
2
3    int main()
4    {
5            FILE *wfile;
6            WINDOW *win;
7
8            initscr();
9            start_color();
10           init_pair(1,COLOR_WHITE,COLOR_RED);
11           refresh();
12
13   /* open file */
14           wfile = fopen("window.win","r");
15           if( wfile==NULL )
16           {
17                   endwin();
18                   puts("Error reading file");
19                   return(1);
20           }
21
22   /* read window's data */
23           win = getwin(wfile);
24           fclose(wfile);
25           wrefresh(win);
26           getch();
27
28           endwin();
29           return(0);
30   }
```

The file `window.win` is opened at Line 14. It's created by the code in example `15-06-wputfile.c`.

Line 23 reads the data from `window.win` and assigns it the window variable `win`. The *getwin()* function not only reads in the data, but it creates the window, which is displayed at Line 25.

Yes, the window was saved as a blue window, but it appears red when the program is run. That's because the attribute saved with the text is `COLOR_PAIR(1)`. The color combination for `COLOR_PAIR(1)` is set differently in the new program, so the color used is different. This is the only text attribute that changes; everything else about the window is the same as it was saved, including its location on the screen.

Also by Dan Gookin

Check out these other titles available from Dan Gookin at the Amazon Kindle store:

Beginning Programming with C For Dummies

Android Phones For Dummies

Android Tablets For Dummies

Word 2016 For Dummies

Word 2016 For Professionals For Dummies

PCs For Dummies

Laptops For Dummies

Check out my website for all current titles:
http://www.wambooli.com/titles/

Printed in Great Britain
by Amazon

47625451R00088